LEGAL PRACTICE HANDBOOK

LEGAL
RESEARCH
Law-Finding and Problem-Solving

LEGAL PRACTICE HANDBOOK

LEGAL RESEARCH

Law-Finding and Problem-Solving

Victor Tunkel, Barrister

Senior Lecturer in Law
Queen Mary & Westfield College, University of London

Series Editor: Anthony G. King, MA, Solicitor
Director of Education, Clifford Chance

BLACKSTONE PRESS LIMITED

First published in Great Britain 1992 by Blackstone Press Limited, 9–15 Aldine Street, London W12 8AW. Telephone 081–740 1173

© Victor Tunkel, 1992

ISBN: 1 85431 171 9

British Library Cataloguing in Publication Data
A CIP catalogue record for this book is available from the British Library

Typeset by Style Photosetting Ltd, Mayfield, East Sussex
Printed by BPCC Wheatons Ltd, Exeter

Contents

Preface

It is customary in a foreword to thank colleagues for the help they have given towards the book in inspiring the author's first thoughts and correcting his first efforts; to which one always adds that any faults which remain are the author's alone. All this I freely acknowledge. But it has to be said that those who have most inspired me to think about law-finding as a subject have done so by their requests for help: academics and students needing assistance with their research; solicitors with responsibility for trainees; course-planners for the Inns of Court School of Law's new vocational course; to which I should add the steady stream of inquirers into legal history who have sought my help as Secretary of the Selden Society.

The book itself however, would not have been written but for practical experience in training sessions at several leading firms of solicitors, in talking to law librarians and in writing for the Bar School's course manuals. Above all, the feedback from instructing new lawyers has helped me to appreciate what they need to know and given me some idea how to engage them in law-finding. To all of these I give my thanks.

As part of formal legal training, research technique is a new subject in this country. Efforts to teach or write about it are likely to have all the shortcomings of pioneering ventures, so corrections and suggestions for improvement would be more than usually welcome. I only ask that readers more knowledgeable than I will remember that it is mainly beginners' research skills that I am trying to develop, the locating of the basic building-materials of the law, and the deploying of these to resolve everyday practical problems.

I would like to thank the Blackstone Press and the series editor for their encouragement of such an uncertain subject (and author), to which I would add my admiration — working as I do for what has to be the most conservative of law-publishers — for their fresh and enterprising approach. Finally I thank my wife for letting me monopolise our word-processor for a long period and for her patience over an even longer one.

Victor Tunkel
October 1992

Introduction

THE AIM OF THIS BOOK

This book is an attempt to fill a small but remarkable gap in the traditional education of English lawyers. If you ask experienced practitioners how they learned to tackle legal problems and to find the appropriate law, the chances are they will say 'trial and error', 'hit and miss', 'jumping in at the deep end', or similar vague expressions. The probability is that they never actually 'learned' it at all, in the sense of being taught. Even today, when the profession's educators are at long last beginning to give due emphasis to vocational skills, very few law students get much systematic instruction or testing in the ability to use the daily, routine, apparatus of the law; and in the technique of legal problem-solving.

It is a small gap because, as with other lawyers' skills, the competent young practitioner does slowly acquire and sharpen these tools in practice. It is nevertheless lamentable that until recently neither branch of the profession's law schools has thought it necessary to attempt to teach even the rudiments of legal research technique. As for the universities, they pile heavy loads of legal doctrine on their students, expecting them to absorb, criticise and apply it to problem situations. But almost all this material is pre-packaged and presented to students by way of textbooks, casebooks, lectures and recommended articles. By use of these alone, undergraduates are able to perform all the tasks required of them. Rarely are they expected to *find out* the law for themselves. Even if they are, few academic law libraries have the specialised materials which the practitioner needs to use.

The result is that generations of young barristers and solicitors have arrived at their first job without any real training in what is one of its most essential functions. They have then been expected to 'pick it up' as best they can. Some never do, or perhaps succeed without ever having to, if they find a niche in areas of practice where research and problem-solving play little part. If such limited practice is possible today, it must surely confine one to the least interesting and stimulating work. At all events, every young would-be lawyer should as a matter of self-respect and professional pride want to acquire skill in tackling legal problems and so merit membership of a learned profession.

THE INTENDED READER

This book is mainly aimed at those just starting out on their career in the law. They have their law degree or equivalent and have completed their professional law course. They now face their first real out-of-classroom legal encounters. Some areas of law encountered may be familiar, others entirely new. The practitioners' law library and resources are almost wholly new and daunting. The clients' facts they are expected to unravel and opine upon are not tidily pre-selected as were problem facts presented to them in the classroom; and it may not be obvious what is the precise legal question the facts pose.

THE TEACHING OF RESEARCH SKILLS

To some extent, the barren educational landscape described above is now changing. The Council of Legal Education, in the new vocational course begun at the Bar School in 1989, introduced some legal research content into its curriculum. Likewise the Law Society's new course, beginning in 1993, puts the emphasis on lawyers' skills. The problem for any such courses, however, is the difficulty of teaching a subject of this sort *en masse*. It really calls for small-group instruction, in or close to the participants' law library, with some individual attention to each student's thought processes and strategies. I hope therefore that the present book may, in addition to helping individual law students and trainees to become familiar with the sources of legal knowledge and the technique of problem solving, also assist legal trainers in their planning of in-house courses. Ultimately, it must be said, there are limits to what any mere book can do when it comes to skills which can only be fully acquired and developed in practice. But we all have to start somewhere. . . .

THE ARRANGEMENT OF THIS BOOK

(a)   An opening look at the nature of legal problems, contrasting the academic with the practical.

(b)   Surveys of basic resources, with exercises on each to gain familiarity.

(c)   Suggestions for how to make and retain notes of researches.

(d)   More advanced problem–solving.

(e)   More advanced resources and exercises.

(f)   Being and keeping up to date.

(g)   Researching non-UK law.

(h)   Computerised resources.

(i)   Diagrams to indicate searching sequences.

(j)   End-of-course self-assessment.

(k)   Suggested solutions to exercises.

(l)   Further reading.

(m)   Index.

TO REPEAT OR TO CROSS-REFER?

As you progress through this book you will find that some things seem to get repeated. There are good reasons for this. The first is that the lawyer's working tools and resources have initially to be described as static apparatus on the library shelf; and then looked at again in a more functional way when they are put to work in problem-solving. Secondly, there is a great deal of information for the beginner to have to take in and retain; repetition acts as a welcome reminder. Thirdly, legal research is itself a repetitive process and skill develops only with familiarity, i.e., repetition.

The alternative to repetition is that necessary evil of the law searcher's existence, cross-referencing. In this book, I have tried to strike a convenient balance, preferring to repeat or restate things where I thought this would be more helpful than sending you back for them; but otherwise to cross-refer. I hope readers will find both the repetitions and the cross-referencing appropriate, or at any rate not too tiresome.

Chapter One

First Steps in Problem Solving

1.1 THE APPROACH TO LEGAL PROBLEMS

If you are a young lawyer on the threshold of practice, you will already have been tackling legal problems academically for some years. You have now to make the transition to the different technique involved in dealing with practitioners' legal problems. What is the difference?

1.2 PROBLEMS IN LAW STUDIES AND IN PRACTICE

The sort of problems you have encountered so far may have involved very intricate questions of law. But —

(a) The facts were always selected for you, whereas in real-life the facts are a mass of disorganised raw material which you have to sort out.

(b) The facts you were given were indisputable, whereas in real-life litigation the facts are almost always uncertain until the court 'finds' them – too late for the lawyer's advice.

(c) In typical academic problems, there are unknown, non-given, facts which are unascertainable. You were expected to speculate on these and come to a hypothetical statement of the law, whereas in real life you are expected to find out, to extract from the client all the further information which you have first to identify as relevant.

(d) The problems you have had up to now, however difficult, were always in an area of law that you had under study, whereas the practitioner may often have to venture into totally unknown or new areas of law.

To see how this difference works out in practical terms, we can start from familiar ground, a problem situation which should be well within your existing knowledge:

> Lady Frail employed Drainrod Ltd, plumbers and heating con-
> tractors, to modernise the elderly central heating system in her
> stately home. Hazard, one of the Drainrod workmen, while using
> a blowlamp on some pipes, accidentally set fire to a priceless
> tapestry hanging on the wall. The fire was soon put out and only
> very slight damage done. Drainrod Ltd's insurers have agreed to
> pay the cost of specialist repairs to the tapestry. However, Lady
> Frail, who was present and saw what happened, collapsed and had
> to be resuscitated. She has been confined to her room ever since,
> suffering, she says, from headaches, nightmares, depression, loss
> of appetite and fear of going out. She is claiming heavy damages
> from Drainrod Ltd for her illness.

Drainrod Ltd's insurers ask your advice. They say that if Hazard was careless (which has not been admitted), Lady Frail was warned to remove the tapestries for their safety before the work began and she had refused to do so; and that even assuming her symptoms were genuine and not exaggerated, she is asking for damages for personal injuries when what happened did not put her or anyone else in danger.

How should any lawyer, academic or practising, go about research-ing in order to advise? By going through the following stages:

1.2.1 Analysis

Every fact-situation has a mass of raw facts most of which are for legal purposes immaterial. From these the lawyer has to extract the really significant facts which trigger the law. This case could be about central heating installation. An insurance policy is involved. So is health and safety at work. The national heritage might come into it if, for example, the tapestry had been accepted by the Revenue in lieu of inheritance tax. Or is it about regulations for the use of blowlamps? Vicarious liability? Remoteness of damage? None of these?

1.2.2 Classification

If you reject these as starting points it is because you know enough law to classify this problem as in the general area of negligence, duty of care, nervous shock, acceptance of risk, contributory negligence, and so forth. Of course you may actually know the relevant law from your tort studies, but if you do not, or you want confirmation, you would presumably go to your textbook and find the answer there, or at least a pointer towards it. The practising lawyer would do much the same thing, except that it would be a very different sort of text book that would be used.

But now suppose the unlikely: that your tort course did not include liability for nervous shock. Provided that you could recognise the problem as lying somewhere in the general area of negligence liability, or at least tort, you could still find the answer by persistent searching in the textbooks covering those branches of the law.

1.2.3 Cold starting

If, however, you were unable to say with confidence which branch of the law might be involved and were starting from cold, where should you look? Is there some sort of general comprehensive indexed work which has the whole of English law in it? Or is that too much to hope? There is indeed such a treasure in the law library. We will look at it later. But at this stage you should appreciate that if you have to start from scratch, you will need to think of some suitable word or phrase or legal term or other point of entry which a reference work can recognise; and that a work of that sort must have some system of constantly revising the information it gives out if it is to be reliable, which you must know how to operate.

To return to our problem, you should from your textbook or further research eventually find a reference to *Attia* v *British Gas plc* [1988] QB 304, [1987] 3 All ER 455, [1987] 3 WLR 1101. In a footnote, perhaps, you are told that this says that damages are recoverable for nervous shock even though no human being is endangered and the shock arises from fear merely for property.

1.2.4   Following through

You now feel that you have the answer to the problem, or at least to the major point of principle. You should of course find the case report from the references given and see exactly what it says. If it seems relevant, you would then begin to construct your argument either to bring the *Lady Frail* case within it, or to try to get around it, as required. But you might be wasting your time if you did this without first checking any supplements, addenda, stop press, etc., to the sources you have used in case, for example, the rule in *Attia* has been reversed on appeal, or overruled, or otherwise affected by more recent legal happenings.

Alternatively, when you found the *Attia* case cited, there might have been attached to the citation a footnote of the sort that frequently appears:

> See also now Firetools (Precautions against Accidents) (Safety Modifications) Regulations 1992, SI 1992 No. 4236 (implementing Council Directive 1990/677).

This sounds as if it could be important, but what exactly is it, and how would you find it?

1.2.5   Final update

Even supposing the *Attia* case is the only authority cited and you checked any supplements and found nothing further, can you be sure it is still good law? Was there not a recent House of Lords' decision on the whole question of nervous shock? Did it overrule, or limit, or confirm, or not even mention *Attia*? How do you find out if there has been such a case, not knowing its name?

1.2.6 Further commentary

Cases and statutes and committee reports and other legal effusions which are of any importance never go unremarked by learned commentators and professional opinion. What has been written about the *Attia* case by legal pundits could well help to shape your advice. How can you track down all such writings?

Summary

The above example is meant to illustrate most of the main stages in legal research: analysis, classification or keywording, decoding references, following through, accessing familiar and unfamiliar sources, updating and surveying current opinion. In this book you will find all of these explained, with exercises on each for you to improve your skill.

1.3 TYPES OF LEGAL PROBLEM

Problems presented to the lawyer in practice can involve just about anything. Those which are not really about law at all (financial, medical, family, political or whatever) need to be recognised early and the client appropriately redirected. Genuine legal posers can be broadly subdivided into focused and unfocused problems.

1.3.1 Focused problems

In these the questions are formulated. At their simplest, they consist of such queries as what is the maximum sentence, the period of notice required, the appropriate form, the relevant public body, the limitation period, and so forth. The answers may still be elusive, but at least the question (assuming it is the right question) is clearly posed.

Still focused but slightly harder to find is the type of problem where we know (or think we know) the law but want the authority for it: for example, everyone knows that the standard rate of income tax is 25 per cent, or that you can lop off your neighbour's overhanging branches, or that a deed no longer has to be under seal, but where are these things laid down? The task is to classify the proposition of law to its appropriate context and to search there. None of these examples should take long to back with authority.

1.3.2   Unfocused problems

These are the truer test of the lawyer's perception and skill. From a mass of raw information (including documents and clients' assertions of purported fact) the lawyer has first to recognise and select the significant facts in order to arrive at the legal issue. Faulty analysis will lead to a mis-formulation and thence to an answer, perhaps correct, to the wrong question. Sound analysis of the raw material, identifying the legal issues, brings the problem into focus so that it is then susceptible to sound research technique. The *Lady Frail* case above is an example of a simple unfocused problem and, as we saw, the process is not so different, at least initially, from that in which you should have been tackling hypothetical problems set in your law courses: a set of facts had to be analysed, then the appropriate legal rules sought, then the rules applied to the given facts and the resulting 'advice' offered.

As to the differences between the student's and the practising lawyer's exertions which we noted, in this book the problems are inevitably academic in that they have pre-determined facts; and they are also misleading in that they all have definite and ascertainable answers, something real-life law does not always provide. However, for learning purposes these are necessary and desirable artificialities.

1.4   INTO THE UNKNOWN

There was the other difference we noted between academic and real-life legal problems. From the day you begin in practice you will be faced with problems calling for research in totally new areas. (Even those you thought you knew something about will somehow seem different.)

If you are really stone cold and cannot see where to start, do not despair. Make a careful examination of the facts and see whether you can extract any keywords. These are any terms, words or phrases which may be legally significant and therefore index-worthy (or LEXIS-worthy, but more on that later). The broadest general index in the law library is the Consolidated Index to *Halsbury's Laws of England*. This multi-volume work is an encyclopaedia of all the law of England in whatever form and on whatever subject. Of course that is an ambition which can never be achieved, but the set (described further below 2.3.1) goes a good way towards it; and its two volumes of Consolidated Index (Vols 55 and 56) are the most comprehensive printed word index of English law. Their great merit is that they do not require you to classify into legal concepts but rather come to meet you at a very low level of minutiae. For example, opening it at random, on one page of index we find

. . . *go-cart, gold, Gold Coast, golden handshake, golf club, gonorrhoea, good behaviour, Good Friday*. . . .

More will be said about this *Halsbury* set later. For the present have a look at its alphabetical subject-matter arrangement and in particular at the index volumes. Note that in common with other multi-volume sets, this has an annual *Cumulative Supplement, Current Service* and *Noter-Up*, which keep the whole set up to date and which must always be checked in following through.

Here are some focused problems, which are intended to be in unfamiliar territory, yet which are easily solvable just by using the *Halsbury* index, the appropriate subject volume and annual supplement volume. You should manage to do each of these in about five to ten minutes. The answers are in Chapter 19.

EXERCISE A   FOCUSED FIVE-MINUTE PROBLEMS

1.   When is the close season for snipe?

2.   Must London taxis have meters?

3.   In what circumstances may a Coroner hold an inquest on a Sunday?

4.   If the police tow away a car abandoned in the street, can they sell it?

5.   At what time(s) of day may a loudspeaker be used in the street for purposes of advertising or selling?

6. North Sea gas is odourless but when it comes into our houses it smells. In legal terms, why?

7. For how long is the protection of a registered design granted? For how long may that initial protection be extended?

8. Certain articles are required by law to be hallmarked but are not required to have a date letter. Which?

9. Why are there quarter-mile posts all along the railway track?

10. Mary failed her driving test. She thinks she should have passed. Can she, in law, do anything?

Answering some, if not all of these, and quite quickly, should give you confidence to try your hand at a few unfocused problems which follow.

EXERCISE B   SIMPLE UNFOCUSED PROBLEMS

1. John and his wife Mary, both aged 61, went to play bowls at the local bowling green run by the Council. A notice stated that admission was free for senior citizens. Mary, who got her pension when 60, therefore got in free. John, not being pensionable until 65, had to pay £1. John says that he feels he is being made to pay just because he is a man. He wants to know if they can do this.

Analysis: The first thing to do is to see if there is a legal problem here at all. It may be an area of law you have studied, in which case you will be able to spot which facts may be significant. Assuming, however, it is unfamiliar, you need to exercise your lawyer's instinct and see whether any law could be involved and, if so, in what sort of area.

However blank you may feel on the particular topic, you know more than you may think you do. Your legal training should have given you sufficient foundation to be able to identify the likely area of law. In the last resort, do it by elimination. Is it about pension rights? These concern, e.g., who is entitled, at what age, to how much, contributions, deductions, etc. It is common knowledge that women get their retirement pension at 60 whereas men go on earning until 65. The Council are only acknowledging that fact of life. Well, it concerns husband and wife. But is that relevant here? Would it matter if they were not married, or were two men? How about freedom of contract? Can a Council charge and not charge different classes of user as it sees fit? Is it about local government law? Would it be different if it were not a municipal facility but one run by, e.g., a public sporting body? Is it about sex discrimination? Does that apply here, where it is the man, not the woman, who is the 'victim'? Is it about the law relating to bowling greens?

Having stirred up the dust, let it settle and see if any one or more of these suggestions looks promising to you. Assuming, as we have, that the area is new to you, what we have been doing is to clutch at each of the salient terms in the facts to see whether these (or any reformulation of them) might be useful as a keyword with which to unlock the problem: 'pension', 'bowling green', 'sex discrimination', etc. If one of these sounds to you much more likely than the others, you could be right, and half way to finding the answer. It is in fact to be found in a fairly recent House of Lords' decision.

It must be said that the keyword approach will not always work; not, at least, without some further ingenuity on your part. However, this will be looked at again later in more advanced researching. For the present, we can continue with a few more problems where keywords will work:

2. A monthly magazine for law students is thinking of running a competition. Readers are invited to guess the number of Finals candidates in the forthcoming exam who will pass in all subjects. Entry is free. Only one entry is allowed for each reader, who must be a Finals candidate. If no one gets the right figure, the prize (choice of the *White Book* or *Archbold*) will go to the closest guess. The magazine would like your confirmation that they can go ahead.

Analysis: What keywords or key areas of law are here? Press freedom and censorship law? Competition law? Prize law? Betting and Lotteries? None of these sounds very likely, but with a little persistence you should get the answer.

3. Your client telephones you for urgent advice. After last night's severe storm, the roof and upper part of his house are in a semi-detached state. His surveyor has advised that they are dangerous and must be pulled down without delay. Workmen are standing by to do it but the house is a listed building and the work has not been authorised. Can the client go ahead or what should he do?

Analysis: One obvious keyword or key concept here which should point you straight at the appropriate branch of the law.

4. Jane was left property by the will of her husband Peter who died last October. Peter's will, made in November 1982 when he and Jane were engaged, stated that he was looking forward to marrying Jane. He did marry her in March 1983. She now seeks advice as to her rights under the will. She has been told by Peter's family that she gets nothing under the will because her marriage to Peter revoked it.

Analysis: No difficulty in finding the area of law but it needs close attention to the facts, dates, etc., in finding and applying the relevant authorities.

5. Helen moved into a flat on the top floor of a converted Victorian house outside London. It had sash windows with deep stone sills. She put out on her two windowsills plastic containers with her favourite daffodil bulbs. A passing policeman rang her door bell and when she went down he told her she was committing an offence and must remove the containers. Helen was indignant and refused politely to take the containers inside. The policeman arrested her. Advise her whether she might indeed have committed an offence, as the policeman said; and, if so, whether he was lawfully arresting her.

Analysis: When Helen tells you all this, you will first have to try and extract the vital matters from the non-material facts. But what you consider vital will to some extent depend on your initial ideas, classified, however vaguely. In real life Helen would of course be informed at an early stage of the offence alleged against her, which you could then check up on. Nevertheless try this one starting cold, just for the exercise.

Suggested solutions to the above problems are in Chapter 19 together with some further discussion of method. Note your answers carefully and also the way you got to them. If you didn't succeed in getting an answer, note what point you reached and see whether you were going along the right lines or not. Remember that in legal research everyone, even the most experienced lawyers, makes mistakes or false starts which lead nowhere. The important thing is to learn from these so that you develop a lawyer's instinct for effective research.

Chapter Two

The Lawyer's Resources

2.1 THE LIBRARY

Law libraries differ greatly in size and content, according to the differing needs of their users.

2.1.1 Academics', practitioners' and reference libraries

Until now any law library you have used is likely to have been an academic library, strong perhaps in reports, statutes, academic periodicals, and historical and philosophical works, but not so strong on practitioners' materials. Practitioners need a different sort of legal literature: textbooks which have vastly more detailed law, every known specific instance rather than speculation or criticism, and periodicals on highly specialised areas of practice appropriate to the particular firm. So the first thing you must do is familiarise yourself with your office or chambers' library. Find out what it has and where it has it. Then find out which library, e.g., the Law Society's or your Inn's, the Institute of Advanced Legal Studies in London or your local Law Society's library in the provinces, you can use for reference when yours has not got what you need, and then have a look at that library too. Please read carefully what follows, and use it as a *guidebook to the shelves*, finding and exploring each of the materials described. This is especially important for those trainees who do not have law degrees. Law graduates may find some of the information pretty basic. Even so, it will not harm them to be reminded and to have their knowledge made more systematic.

2.1.2 The exercises

Merely looking at the shelves, and perhaps flicking through a few books taken down at random, will not do much for you. Do the simple exercises at the end of each section so as to get some basic dexterity with each of the sources in turn.

2.1.3 The essential parts of a law library

An English law library of whatever sort has to have at least five different sorts of materials: statutes, reports, journals, textbooks, and general reference works. Of these, statutes and law reports are sometimes called primary sources because their content, legislation and precedent, is the law; whereas the other secondary sources, e.g., textbooks or *Halsbury's Laws*, though they may often be highly regarded, are only their writers' opinion of what the law is. Here at the outset we see an important difference between law studies and law practice: it may have earned you points in tutorial to cite and rely on a statement in a textbook or article, but it will rarely suffice in court.

2.2 THE NEW TECHNOLOGY

We must get used to thinking of the books on the shelves as *hard-copy*, by contrast with:

(a)   Micro-reproduction: in the years to come more and more of the big sets of law serials will be reduced to microform, compact disc or other electronic storage; and

(b)   Computerised sources: many lawyers have LEXIS and some also have access to other databases. To use these you will need to have a special course of instruction. There are some suggestions later on the approach to using LEXIS, and a mention of other databases you may meet, but otherwise these notes deal mainly with what is on the shelf. In any event you must master the lawyer's traditional tools first.

2.3 BEING UP TO DATE

More than any other professional, the practising lawyer has to be right up to date: aware of this morning's newspaper law reports, this afternoon's statements in Parliament. When it comes to research, the need to find very recent law arises in various ways: for example, one may be prompted by a vague recollection that there was something about this not long ago, which ought to be chased up. But we have to be more methodical than this and thoroughly update everything we find before relying on it. We have to get into the good habit of automatically following through with our research each time. This will be mentioned later under each source. But we need to know something about updating in general.

2.3.1 Sequential searching

When we used *Halsbury's Laws* in the first exercises, we saw that this multi-volume set has several components: various general index volumes, main subject volumes, annual *Cumulative Supplement, Current Service* parts and a *Noter-Up*. With this, as with any of the other multi-volumes sets, you must always follow through in sequence with your research. The procedure may vary slightly according to which work you are using. The three *Halsbury* sets, the two precedent encyclopaedias, the *Current Law* service and many of the multi-volume textbooks are arranged for some sort of sequential accessing. The way to do it, if not obvious, is usually explained somewhere at the beginning of the first volume, or in a separate booklet provided with the set.

Broadly speaking, the sequence is:

main volume ➡ annual supplement ➡ loose-leaf service

It is very simple, quickly done, and often turns up nothing. (This is usually good news, because it should mean that the law we have found in the main volume continues to be reliable.) More to the point, it is lazy not to do it; and there is nothing more embarrassing than to base your thinking and advising on what the main volume says only to find later that it has been totally overthrown by something you could and should have found in the supplement.

For a topical illustration of this which has a certain irony, anyone wanting to discover the principles of property valuation for local taxation purposes, starting from scratch, could well find themselves directed to *Halsbury's Laws of England*, Vol. 39. At the time of writing, Vol. 39 gives the scheme for valuation under the General Rates Act 1967. But this is all about old-fashioned rating which we all know has gone forever, so we hasten to the *Cumulative Supplement*. That tells us that the 1967 Act is repealed and that the Local Government Finance Act 1988 is now the ruling statute, giving us a new scheme called (officially) the Community Charge. The Act says that hereditaments are not valued any more save where non-domestic. But continuing to the *Current Service* volume we find that the Local Government Finance and Valuation Act 1991 has in turn begun to dismantle the Community Charge, to replace it by yet a further scheme, the Council Tax. This will restore property-based valuations and for this purpose s. 3 provides for detailed new regulations for the valuation of property according to bands. At the time of writing, however, the Local Government Finance Act 1992 has just arrived, and it repeals the 1991 Act. . . .

In due course – perhaps by the time you are reading this – the next annual *Cumulative Supplement* will have appeared and will have absorbed the more recent *Current Service* contents and still more recent happenings. And eventually a replacement Vol. 39 may be issued to start the process all over again but meantime this illustration shows the steady and never-ending accumulation of new law being added stage by stage to the multi-volume works, and the importance of scanning these methodically through their various component parts, and then trying to get a final and complete update.

2.3.2 Know your source's date

A useful discipline is always to remember to look for the effective date of the book or reference source you are using. Bound volumes will state it somewhere near the front – though rarely as prominently as they should. That should alert you to the need not only for updating, but also as from when. Loose-leaf volumes have each new section inserted by the librarian, who will confirm doing so, with the date, usually on a card at the back of the binder. Remember that this date of insertion may be a month or more after the latest section was edited.

2.4 *CURRENT LAW*

When it comes to updating, the best all-round set of tools on the library shelf are those provided by the *Current Law* service. These are more fully described in 13.3 but as *Current Law* is a postscript to every sort of law, we should look at it briefly now.

2.4.1 The monthly parts

These blue booklets give all the month's law, of whatever sort, digested under subject headings. Each new monthly part also has indexes of cases and statutes and other things; and these monthly indexes take in all the previous months' indexes, going back to January, so you only have to look at the latest monthly part to access the whole year's issues down to then. Have a look at the latest issue's subject index, at the back of the booklet. You will find citations such as 'Feb 250' or 'Apr 372', giving the paragraph numbers of those earlier issues under which the legal happening is digested.

2.4.2 The *Citators*

The spin-off of the monthly *Current Law* are the two citators, *Current Law Legislation Citator* and *Current Law Case Citator*. These give every happening to, respectively, every Act (of whatever date) and every reported case (of whatever date) if the happening occurred between 1947 and the end of last year. The latest blue monthly part then continues these citations for the present year with any such happenings up to the end of last month.

That is as much as you need to note at this stage about *Current Law* (save perhaps for a word of warning about the alleged joke that appears on the top of the first page each month!). We will meet the service frequently and can begin to put it to work. We go to the shelves now, to look first at 'the law', legislation and precedent, in the forms in which it appears there.

Chapter Three

Legislation

3.1 PRIMARY AND SECONDARY LEGISLATION

3.1.1 Primary legislation

Legislation may be primary or secondary. In the United Kingdom primary legislation takes the form of statutes which today are Acts of Parliament. Acts are either Public General Acts, Local Acts, or Private and Personal Acts. Of all of these the only ones of importance for everyday practice are Public General Acts, which make up what is sometimes called our 'statute book'.

3.1.2 Secondary legislation

Secondary legislation, referred to as 'subordinate' or 'delegated', consists of law which has the full force of statute but which has been laid down not by Parliament itself but by lesser bodies authorised by Parliament. Thus local authorities and public utilities are often given power to make by-laws. (For how to find local by-laws, see Local Government Act 1972, s. 236, as amended.) For present purposes we need consider only Statutory Instruments, in which form the regulations made by government departments are published. We will look at these in later chapters. First we must look at the more basic sources.

3.2   ACTS OF PARLIAMENT

As serials, these appear in law libraries in three main forms:

3.2.1   Queen's Printer's copies

3.2.1.1   *Status*

These are the officially issued Acts in the form in which they were passed by Parliament. For citation and use in court, these are the only versions the judges wish to refer to.

3.2.1.2   *Publication*

Each new Act on getting the Royal Assent is published by Her Majesty's Stationery Office (HMSO), whose head is also known as the Queen's Printer of Acts of Parliament. Your library may have some or all of these as one-off copies of individual Acts as issued by HMSO. More conveniently, on the library shelf these Acts will be found in bound volumes with either *Public General Acts and Measures* or *Law Reports Statutes* on the spine. Inside, both these series are identical Queen's Printer's copies. (The apparent contradiction of *Law Reports Statutes* is simply explained: the publishers of the *Law Reports* offer the year's statutes as an optional extra in the library's annual subscription to their reports and are authorised to put their name on them as if their publisher.)

3.2.1.3   *Local and Personal Acts*

These are also published by HMSO but separately from the Public Acts. Only specialised reference libraries are likely to have all of them though ordinary law libraries may have indexes which give their names and numbers. Each year's Local and Personal Acts are listed in the last annual bound volume of Queen's Printer's copies. From 1992 *Current Law Statutes* (see below) has the texts of Local and Personal Acts.

3.2.1.4   *Format*

HMSO now publishes Queen's Printer's copies of Acts in A4 paper size. Current one-off copies in the library will be this size.

Fortunately the bound volumes are still supplied in the traditional and much more convenient size.

3.2.2 Annotated statutes

Most libraries have *Current Law Statutes Annotated*, an optional further part of the *Current Law* service. These also are arranged in annual volumes like the Queen's Printer's copies, with very recent Acts arriving in loose-leaf booklets during the year. *Current Law Statutes* have annotations almost throughout. These are helpful (but unofficial) inserted notes and comments. The annotations, written by specialist editors, give much information on, e.g., the legal and Parliamentary background; cases, regulations, or other statutes affecting each section; and often a general running commentary. For research purposes annotated statutes are much more useful than the bare official versions.

3.2.3 Classified annotated statutes

Halsbury's Statutes (not to be confused with *Halsbury's Laws of England*) are not only annotated but arranged within a multi-volume set in alphabetical order of subject headings. The set thus organises in its many volumes the entire statute law of this country, of whatever date, which is still to any extent in force. The fourth edition (grey with red labels) is now almost complete. The whole set is kept up to date to the beginning of the present year by an annual *Cumulative Supplement*. Find this (it occupies two volumes) and see how it follows the same sequence of volumes and subject headings as the main set. For still more recent developments there is a loose-leaf *Noter-Up* volume; and this has dividers within it to show the various updating functions it performs. Then there is a series of loose-leaf volumes called *Current Statutes Service*: these give the text of Acts too recent to get into the appropriate bound volume. Completing the set there is a separate index volume which lists both alphabetically and chronologically every Act extant with its reference in the main set, or in the *Current Statutes Service*, indicated by a letter S. This index volume also has a subject index covering the whole set, and this is additional to the subject-index which is at the back of each individual volume.

3.2.4 Using these annotations

Notice how the annotators' approach differs in the *Current Law Statutes* and in *Halsbury's*. The *Current Law* style is informative, discursive and often critical. *Halsbury's* commentary is purely formal, restricted to the meanings of terms, cross-references, and so forth. However *Halsbury's Statutes* have the advantage as the years go by that they are reissued with their annotations updated, whereas the *Current Law* series remain with their commentaries as when first published; and as mentioned before, the *Halsbury* set has all the statutes which are in force, whereas *Current Law Statutes* annual volumes began only in 1949.

3.2.5 Very new Acts

Annotations take time to prepare. It may be some while before the edited *Current Law* or *Halsbury* version of an Act arrives. (Meantime they may issue a temporary unannotated version on coloured paper.) During that delay you will have only the HMSO version of a brand new Act to consult, and will have to do your own interpreting unaided. If so, remember that there is often a lot of helpful commentary by the profession on a Bill during its passage through Parliament. This may be found in the practitioners' journals. See for these 9.1–9.2.

3.3   CITATION OF STATUTES

3.3.1   By title

Every modern Act of Parliament has a short title and year e.g., Financial Services Act 1986. The Act gives itself its short title, usually in its last numbered section. (It is called a *short* title to distinguish it from the *long* title, an old, traditional, style of heading the Act. You will see that this may run to many lines and is of little use either as a title or for anything else.)

3.3.2   By chapter number

Every Act is given a unique 'chapter' number within its year. For example, the Act 1986 c. 60 is another way of referring to the

Financial Services Act of that year. The chapter number has no significance except to tell us that it was the 60th Act passed in 1986 and to distinguish it from any other Act which might have a similar short title. Before 1963, chapter numbers were based on the regnal year or years of the sovereign's reign during which the session of Parliament which passed the Act took place. We then passed the Acts of Parliament Numbering and Citation Act 1962. This (though still calling itself 10 & 11 Eliz 2, c. 34) changed the system from the beginning of 1963 to the present method of citation by chapter number in the calendar year, as shown for the 1986 Act above. Local and Personal Acts are numbered in the same way but in a separate series. To show this, Local Acts have a Roman numeral e.g., the Port of London Act 1968 is 1968 c. xxxii. Personal Acts have an italic numeral e.g., 1982 c. *2* is the Hugh Small and Norma Small (Marriage Enabling) Act 1982.

3.4 LOOKING UP STATUTES

3.4.1 Do you know the short title and year?

If so, in the annual bound volume or volumes of HMSO versions (see 3.2.1 above) you will find an alphabetical index of the year's Acts giving the chapter number of each. The Acts are bound in chapter number order. Or you can do the same with the *Current Law Statutes* annual volumes. Always look for the index to these in the last volume for the year, where that year had more than one volume.

3.4.2 You know the short title but are not sure of the year

The alphabetical index volume to *Halsbury's Statutes* will give it. Alternatively, *Current Law Legislation Citator* has at the beginning an alphabetical list of statutes which have been in any way active in the years covered by the *Citator* volumes. (For a fuller description of this *Citator* see 13.6.2.)

3.4.3 You do not know the short title, but do know the year and chapter number

This is a bit unlikely, but may sometimes happen with older statutes. You can find it as in 3.4.1 above if it is a calendar year. If it is a regnal year and you have the HMSO bound volumes, you should be able to find any Act this century by looking at the spines, which give the regnal year as well as the calendar year. For older Acts, check the chronological index in *Halsbury's Statutes* index volume, or in the official two-volume *Chronological Table* (see 3.4.4.2 below).

3.4.4   Is the Act in force?

Once you have found your Act, the next most important thing to find out is whether it is in force. There are really two distinct questions:

3.4.4.1   *Is it YET in force?*

Many Acts have a delayed beginning and are kept wholly or partly in suspense awaiting activation. Having found your Act, the first thing to do is to see if it is in force. The first place to look for that is in the commencement section. Go to the end of the Act and find the last two or three sections (of the Act itself, ignoring any schedules – pronounced 'shedule' – which are often appended at the end of Acts). In almost every modern Act these last sections give the short title, the extent (geographical) of operation, and the date of commencement. This may be the date of enactment (which you can find on the first page of the Act in a bracket immediately after the long title), or a stated date or interval after that; or it may be left to the government department concerned (nominally the Secretary of State, or Her Majesty in Council), to bring it into operation, and in such stages, areas, etc., as it sees fit. If the last, this is done by Commencement Order made in a Statutory Instrument (described in Chapter 5).

It follows that it will often be unclear from the Act itself whether it (or the particular bit that you need) is in force. If so, the simplest way to find out is to refer to *Is It In Force?* This annual volume, part of the *Halsbury's Statutes* set, covers every Act of the last 25 years, and is up to date to the beginning of the present year. Acts are listed alphabetically within their year. So find the year first and then the Act by its short title alphabetically. The entry will then give you the date or dates for the various bits which have been or are to be brought into force.

If the *Is It In Force?* entry says '*not in force*', do not rest content. It may have been activated since your copy of *Is It in Force?* was published. Have a look at the loose-leaf *Noter-Up* volume. You will find an *Is It In Force?* section in the binder. Alternatively (or, better, look here too) *Current Law* latest monthly part has all the commencement dates fixed for Acts so far this year. You are now up to date to sometime last month. The legal weeklies (*New Law Journal* (NLJ), *Law Society's Gazette* (LSG) and *Solicitors' Journal* (SJ) have a page giving each week's Commencement Orders. To be right up to the minute, HMSO publish a *Daily List* which some libraries take.

Alternative sources are:

(a)   in the loose-leaf binder of *Current Law Statutes* is a table of Legislation not yet in force. This lists alphabetically Acts which have any bits not yet activated. Because it goes back to 1960 it is occasionally more useful than *Is It In Force?* but it is essentially negative in its content and needs to be supplemented by the latest *Current Law* monthly part: see 13.3.1 below.

(b)   a further alternative, and more useful because it gives both a positive and negative indication, is the list of Commencement of Statutes in the *Noter-Up* loose binder to *Halsbury's Laws* (not *Statutes*). This also goes back to the early 1960s, giving every commencement date or saying specifically '*no date*'. Again, in either case, it is necessary to check the weeklies and if possible the *Daily List*.

3.4.4.2   *Is it STILL in force?*

You will feel rather foolish if you have based your deeply researched conclusions on an Act which has, unknown to you, been repealed or substantially amended. There may be no way of telling this from the Act itself. *Halsbury's Statutes* plus its annual *Cumulative Supplement* plus the *Noter-Up* should give you the present status of the Act. Equally good is *Current Law Legislation Citator* which gives every Act's subsequent life history, down to the end of last year. For happenings since, the loose-leaf service volume of *Current Law Statutes* continues the citator into the recent past; or perhaps easier to check is the statute citator section in the latest monthly part of *Current Law*. This, like the service volume of *Current Law Statutes*, continues the *Legislation Citator* volume into the present year.

The most comprehensive source for all statutes' subsequent statutory history is the two-volume *Chronological Table of the Statutes* published by HMSO. This is very helpful with older statutes, but is not issued sufficiently often to help with more recent happenings. The same is true of their *Statutes in Force*, a loose-leaf series which some libraries take. These aim to provide under subject groupings every extant Act and to continually update and amend the texts.

3.5   FINDING OLDER ACTS

You may occasionally have to find an Act which, dating from before 1865, is not in any of the annual volumes of statutes. If it is still in force to any extent, it will be found in *Halsbury's Statutes* by its subject matter or *via* the index volume. Look there first. If it is not there it must have been repealed. You will nevertheless find it listed under its year and chapter number, in the *Chronological Table of the Statutes* (see 3.4.4.2). If it is in italic type there, it is repealed and the entry will give the repealing Act. If it is in bold type, the Act or some part of it is still in force, or was at the date of your edition of the *Chronological Table*.

In any event, you can find the original text of an old statute in either of two sets: *Statutes of the Realm*, the official set of huge volumes covering 1235 to 1713, produced by the Record Commission in the 19th century. Not many libraries have these despite the fact that they are the required texts for citation in court (see Interpretation Act 1978, s. 19(1)(b)). Your library is more likely to have a set called *Statutes at Large*. This is actually the name of several different unofficial collections. They are reasonably accurate, and in size and coverage are more useful as well as more widely available.

3.6   OTHER SOURCES OF STATUTES

Other collections of statutes may be found in the library, mainly where Acts relevant to a particular subject or jurisdiction are provided in works written for that area of practice, e.g., *Stone's Justices Manual, Paterson's Licensing Acts*, and the many encyclopaedic text books (*Planning Law, Medical Law*, etc.).

3.7 LEXIS

The text of every Act in force, with amendments to date, should be accessible on the Statutes file. For LEXIS generally, see Chapter 16.

SUMMARY: STATUTE SEARCHING

1. Looking for the words of a specific Act?
   — date known? search the dated volume(s) index.
   — unsure of date? check *Halsbury's Statutes* alphabetical index.

2. Looking for meaning, application of the words?
   — annotations in *Current Law Statutes* or *Halsbury's Statutes* or textbook.

3. Act too recent for sources in 1. or 2.?
   — *Current Law Statutes* Service or *Halsbury's Statutes* Service.

4. Checking whether in force?
   — commencement section; then:
   — *Is It In Force?* and that bit in *Halsbury's Statutes* Service.
   — *Current Law Legislation Citator* and *Current Law* latest monthly.

5. Follow through, using latest supplements, legal weeklies, *Daily List* etc. (for cases on Acts, see Summary to Chapter 4).

EXERCISE C: STATUTES

1. What are the short titles of the following statutes?

   (a) 21 Geo 3 c. 49; (b) 1971 c. 30; (c) 59 & 60 Vict. c. 14.

2. Are the following in force?

   (a) Outer Space Act.

  (b)   Suppression of Religious Houses Act 1539.

  (c)   Law of Property (Miscellaneous Provisions) Act 1989, s. 1.

  (d)   Broadcasting Act 1990, s. 24

3.   What is the punishment prescribed by Piracy Act 1837, s. 2?

4.   What conduct is made illegal by the Chartered Associations Act?

5.   Which marriages are made void by the Royal Marriages Act?

6.   What is the heading to Part VIII of 15 & 16 Geo 5 c. 20?

Chapter Four

Law Reports

Every law library will have series of reports which are general, covering all courts and subjects, and some which are specialised, covering a limited jurisdiction or area of law. There are now many specialised series, some of which are published as part of practitioners' periodicals.

4.1 REFERENCES

The first problem you may encounter is identifying the various series of reports from initials used in citation. You will be familiar with WLR, All ER, and such commonly occurring references. For any initials which you are not sure of, check in one of the following:

Current Law Case Citator
Halsbury's Laws of England, Vol.1
The Digest Cumulative Supplement volume
Legal Journals Index
Index to Legal Citations and Abbreviations
Sweet and Maxwell's Guide to Law Reports and Statutes

4.2 BRACKETS [SQUARE] AND (ROUND)

Where the year is given in square brackets thus; [1990] 1 WLR 270, it is part of the reference. You therefore need page 270 of the particular volume of those reports with that date on the spine; if there were two or more volumes for that year, the reference will indicate the volume number. Most of our standard series of reports use this *square-bracket* method. Where a date is supplied in round brackets, it is just given to you as useful but non-essential information because in such series the publishers give each volume its own volume number in sequence in the set. For example, (1985) 80 Cr App R 117 tells you it was a case in 1985, but you would not need to know the year to find Vol. 80 in sequence on the shelf.

4.3 THE LAW REPORTS

Our major, semi-official series of reports, produced by the legal profession in the guise of the Incorporated Council of Law Reporting, are called simply *The Law Reports*. They started in 1865. Down to 1890 there were various sub-series with varying styles of citations. Now there are just four series:

4.3.1 Appeal Cases

Cited as AC, has reports of the House of Lords and Judicial Committee of the Privy Council.

4.3.2 Chancery

Cited as Ch, contains reports of cases on all matters heard in the Chancery Division and in the Court of Appeal therefrom.

4.3.3 Queen's Bench (formerly King's)

Cited as QB or KB, contains reports of cases in that Division, including its ordinary, commercial, maritime, appellate and review jurisdictions, and in the CA (Civil Division) therefrom; and also decisions of the CA (Criminal Division).

4.3.4 Family

Cited as Fam, containing reports of the Family Division in its ordinary and appellate jurisdiction, and in the CA on appeal therefrom. (Until 1971 this Division was called the Probate, Divorce and Admiralty Division and its reports were cited in a P series.)

4.4 THE AUTHORITY OF *THE LAW REPORTS*

These are our senior series. They are checked by the judges concerned prior to publication. In addition to the usual headnotes, facts, judgments, they usually give a summary of counsel's arguments. This is helpful in ascertaining what points the court took on board in coming to its decision, though it did not mention these expressly; and conversely, what arguments the court may not have adverted to, which could help you to see a way of narrowing the case's impact.

For all these reasons, these are the preferred series for citation in court (see [1991] 1 All ER 352). Their corresponding disadvantage is that they are slow to arrive in the library, even in their unbound parts. To fill this gap lawyers go to one or other of the two series which appear each week.

4.5 THE TWO WEEKLY SERIES

(a)   The Incorporated Council since 1953 have put out a junior series to fill the gap: the *Weekly Law Reports* (WLR). These arrive in paper parts, often within a month or two of a case being decided. They are grouped into three volumes each year: Vols. 2 and 3 contain cases intended to appear in *The Law Reports*. Vol. 1 has the cases which are not to get that further treatment. Each weekly paper part may contain cases destined for Vol. 1 as well as for Vols 2 or 3. Look carefully at the cover to see the exact content.

(b)   Since 1936 Butterworths have published the *All England Law Reports* (All ER). These have usually filled three consecutive volumes a year, but have now expanded to four volumes.

The coverage and style of both these weekly series is very similar. However the headnotes of the WLR are drafted by the judge(s) concerned whereas those of the All ER are the work of the reporters.

4.6 INDEXES TO ALL THESE REPORTS

The Law Reports publishes at intervals during the course of each year a cumulative index for the year in a pink booklet. This includes not only the current year's *Law Reports* cases and WLR but also the All ER and several other current series: see its front cover for the list. At the end of each year, these indexes are conflated with those for past years, becoming the (limp) red indexes; and each ten years of these are made into a bound red index volume. These pink and red indexes have the additional virtue of listing any Acts, Statutory Instruments and comparable EC and international law materials which have been the subject of reported cases during the year.

4.7 THE MOST RECENT REPORTS

Almost every day in the broadsheet newspapers (*The Times, Independent, Guardian, Telegraph* (until recently), *Financial Times,* and *Scotsman* (recently); and also in *Lloyd's List*) there are citable law reports. In many law libraries, the librarians extract and file these. Some may be reprinted after two or three weeks in one or more of the practitioners' weeklies (*New Law Journal* (NLJ), *Solicitors' Journal* (SJ), *Law Society's Gazette* (LSG)). These cases, if important, eventually get edited into full-strength law reports but until they do, the newspaper or weekly is the only source. Many, moreover, never get further reported and these newspaper reports remain the sole source. There is now a comprehensive means of accessing them: *Daily Law Reports Index* (DLRI).

4.7.1 *Daily Law Reports Index*

DLRI started in 1986. It appears in red-covered limp-bound parts, cumulated quarterly and ending as annual bound volumes. Every case that has been in any of the above dailies is included, and is now accessible in four or five alternative ways: (1) by the parties' names; and also by the ship's name in shipping cases; (2) by subject-matter, for which several different keywords may be extracted from a case; (3) by any statute, SI, RSC, etc., involved in the case. Every newspaper report of the case will be cited, but before trying to find the newspaper report indicated, turn to: (4) cases digest, containing a useful summary of the facts and decision.

DLRI is up to date to about the last fortnight. It is thus the most up to date permanent serial reference work in the law library. Surprisingly few lawyers (as distinct from librarians) yet seem aware of it. You should familiarise yourself with it at the first opportunity and get to know how it works. You may find that your library takes it as an on-line service rather than, or as well as, hard copy.

4.8 OLDER REPORTS

4.8.1 Continuous Series

There were various continuous series which started in the 19th and ended in the middle of the 20th century: the *Law Journal Reports* (LJ), *Law Times Reports* (LT) and *Times Law Reports* (TLR). One such series survives: *Justice of the Peace Reports* dating from 1837. As their names suggest, these reports originated in lawyers' periodicals or newspapers.

Older reports in these series are easy enough to find as they are in numbered volumes. If you have difficulty it may be either because your reference is not to a report but to an item in the original periodical, published and bound separately; or in the case of a *Law Journal Reports* reference, because of the way the separate sub-series (LJQB, LJCh, LJMC, etc.) are all bound in the same-numbered volumes.

4.8.2 Named Reporters

For much of our legal past, law reporting was left to individual enterprise. At first, lawyers and judges made their own personal collections of cases and some of these eventually got printed and published. Later some lawyers began to do it for a living. Such reports are recognisable by their names e.g., Coke's Reports, Vesey Senior, Meeson and Welsby, etc, or their corresponding initials. Some libraries may have some of these in the original volumes. However, they have been more conveniently collected into 176 volumes as the *English Reports* (ER).

4.8.2.1   *Accessing the English Reports*

(a)   If you have the case name use the last two volumes of the set which are an index of case names. This gives both the original reporter's volume and page, and the volume and page in the ER set.

(b)   If you have the reference but not the case name (e.g., 1 Cl & F 527), there is a chart which comes with the ER set that lists all the reporters by name and initials, and tells you which courts they reported and in which volumes of the ER they appear. Look at the spine of the volume(s) cited and see which includes your reporter's volume reference.

(c)   Citing the *English Reports*: strictly, we do not. The ER is just a rationalised reprint. We still cling to the original reporter's name, volume and page when citing his reports as if we were using the old leather tomes. For this purpose you will find the original pagination preserved in the midst of ER pages by numbers in square brackets in the text.

4.8.3   The *All England Reprint* (All ER Rep)

This somewhat misleadingly-named series selects older cases reported in the LT and LJ reports and from the named reporters ((4.7.1) and (4.7.2) above) which still have practical importance. It is therefore a useful alternative source, especially in smaller modern libraries which may lack the older series.

4.9   TO FIND A SPECIFIC CASE REPORT

If you have absorbed the above information you should with a little practice be able to find any case to which you have the reference. What if the reference turns out to be wrong, or you have a case by name only? You need a comprehensive case index.

An eminent barrister once told me of the experience he had as a pupil on his first day in chambers. He was given a bulky set of papers sent by a firm of solicitors and told to study it and write an opinion. After two days of concentrated study he felt he had grasped the facts and the point of law involved. He then asked one of the older members of the chambers about this point. The senior man reflected for a moment and then said 'I think you will find that point is dealt with in *Fisher and Lightwood*'. The youngster thanked him warmly and went straight to the library where he spent the entire morning looking fruitlessly for the supposed case of *Fisher* v *Lightwood*. Had he known his stuff he would have known that *Fisher & Lightwood* is the name of the standard work on mortgages. But even without such knowledge, he should have been able to discover very quickly that there has never been any reported English case of that name. All that is needed is a comprehensive case name index.

4.9.1 Case name indexes

The most comprehensive index of case names in the library is that of *The Digest*. It now occupies four volumes. You may need this if your named case is very old or is from outside England. (See 11.3.2.) For all practical purposes, however, the most useful index is provided by the citator volumes of the *Current Law* service and by the case index to *Halsbury's Laws*.

4.9.1.1 *Current Law Case Citator*

This lists the names of every case – *of whatever date* – which has had any 'life' (decided, distinguished, followed, not followed, etc.) in the period since 1947. It is arranged alphabetically by case name in two hardback volumes, 1947–76 and 1977–88. Every published report of the case is given, as well as any substantial articles or case notes on it, and where it is digested in *Current Law Year Book* (CLYB). In other words, you have the subsequent case history of every case that has had any. A third volume has been started as from 1989 as a cumulating red booklet. Each year this will grow fatter and will eventually make a third bound volume.

4.9.1.2 *Halsbury's Laws case-index volumes*

This has the advantage over *Current Law Case Citator* that it goes back much further, and so should cover all the noteworthy cases there have ever been irrespective of any recent citation, these being mentioned somewhere in this *Halsbury* set. *Current Law Case Citator* is better where you know it is a case which has had something to say or said about it since 1947, because every such case will be listed, however lightweight.

4.10 TO FIND CASE LAW IN GENERAL

If you know that you need to find cases on a topic or line of authority, the sensible place to look may be the practitioners' textbook, where they should all be mentioned at least in the footnotes. If however you want to know of cases of or since a definite date, try *Current Law Year Book* and the current year's parts, or *Halsbury's Laws Annual Abridgment* volumes; and the annual and recent parts of *Daily Law Reports Index*. All of these have good subject-matter or keywords indexes. We have seen that the most comprehensive subject-matter index in the library, covering all forms of law, is that to *Halsbury's Laws*. However, the widest trawl through just the case law of any date is achieved by searching *The Digest*.

4.10.1 *The Digest*

This is a multi-volume encyclopaedia of case law, organised under subject headings. It was formerly called the *English and Empire Digest* and that name reveals one of its virtues: it digests virtually all the reported cases of the common law world outside USA. It now also includes cases of European Community and Human Rights law. It is slightly complicated to use, because of its copious indexes, tables of contents, replacement and continuation volumes, and its system of numbering cases. It is kept up to date by supplements; but it can be misleading in that it never seems to jettison cases which have been, e.g., overruled in effect by statute, or whole areas of law which are defunct, e.g., copyhold. Nevertheless it is a most valuable source once you have learned how to use it, and provided you are sure that it is instances of precedent that you need. In many libraries it is surprisingly underused. It is particularly useful in the way it extends the library both back in history and sideways in geography: if you have a reference to an old case or to one from beyond England, a glance at *The Digest* via its cases index may save a lot of unnecessary outside research. Detailed researching in *The Digest* will be looked at in Chapter 11.

SUMMARY: CASE SEARCHING

1. Looking for report of named case, no reference?
   Current Law Case Citator; if not there
   The Digest cases index.

2. Case too recent for 1.?
   Current Law latest monthly case list
   DLRI case name index.

3. Looking for recent case, name forgotten?
   DLRI keywords index
   Current Law latest monthly subject-matter index.

4. Looking for any cases on specific statute?
   Current Law Legislation Citator volumes, and latest monthly
   DLRI legislation index
   Law Reports pink and red indexes *Statutes Judicially Considered.*

EXERCISE D: LAW REPORTS

1. What are:

   BCLC, BCC, BWCC, WWR, Co Rep, WN, NILR, Com Cas, EG,
   STC?

Which of them does your library have ?

2. How many reports are there of *Street* v *Mountford* in the House
of Lords?

3. Find the most recent cases in the library on –

   (a) market overt;

   (b) *donatio mortis causa;*

   (c) seizure of an aeroplane because its owners had failed to pay
   airport charges;

(d)   telephone tapping.

4.   What type of goods were involved in *Hurry* v *Mangles* (1808)?

5.   Find a case reported in 1989 that says that for canon law purposes there is no difference between a corpse in a grave and cremated ashes.

Chapter Five

Introducing the Statutory Instruments

The statutory instruments were mentioned earlier, alongside statutes, which are their parents. We need to look at them now as they exist on the library shelf. Later we will see how they are effectively researched.

5.1 PUBLICATION

The statutory instruments are a vast series. Currently there are said to be about 14,000 in force, with a constant flow from Whitehall of new ones, revocations and amendments, adding a further 3,000 each year. The official texts are published as Queen's Printer's copies by HMSO. Many of them are just one sheet of paper. If your library takes these they will have to be carefully filed in sequence somewhere. On the shelf they will be found in more durable form.

5.1.1 Annual volumes

As with the statutes, HMSO publishes annual volumes of statutory instruments in sequence. They fill several large blue volumes each year for which few libraries have the shelf space and especially now that these, like the HMSO statutes, have swelled to A4 format.

5.1.2   *Halsbury's Statutory Instruments*

This set of volumes, arranged alphabetically by subject-matter, lists all the SIs in force. It prints the full texts of only a few, selecting the ones which the editors believe to be those most needed by lawyers and which (unlike, e.g., the Rules of the Supreme Court (RSC)) are not likely to be found elsewhere in the library.

There are three ways of accessing this set. You can search by subject-matter by going direct to the subject volume if you can recognise it, or via the softcover *Consolidated Index*, revised annually. The key by reference number is in Vol.1 of the two loose-leaf service volumes, which has a complete numerical (that is, chronological) list indexing every SI in force up to last year. Thirdly, if you have the name of the SI, you can look it up in the alphabetical index of short titles in the *Consolidated Index*.

The content of each volume is updated by following through to the annual supplement, also in Vol. 1 of the loose-leaf binder; and then to the *Monthly Survey*, further on in the same binder. This *Monthly Survey* is accessed by its own separate *key* section following it in the binder. Finally, the annual *Consolidated Index* of subject-matter is itself kept up to date during the year by a supplementary index at the back of the loose-leaf binder.

5.1.3   Textbooks

As with statutes, the main practitioners' works, especially the loose-leaf encyclopaedic textbooks, should set out, or at least refer you to, the SIs relevant to the scope of the book.

5.1.4   Older SIs and SR & Os

If still in force, they should be at least mentioned in *Halsbury's Statutory Instruments*. For the text of an older instrument some of the big law libraries have the blue HMSO annual volumes going back for years. (The SR & Os which preceded the SIs are in red volumes.) In addition, you may find the set of *Statutory Rules and Orders and Statutory Instruments Revised*. This is a reorganisation under subject headings of all the instruments in force at the end of 1948. There are indexes in the last volume; and the *Table of Government Orders* in a separate volume shows the impact of subsequent instruments.

5.1.5 LEXIS

LEXIS carries all the extant SIs in its SI and STATIS files. We will refer to these later.

5.2 CITATION OF SIs

Every SI is given a unique number in its year, shown as, e.g., 1992/1234, or more fully as SI 1992 No. 1234. (The earlier series, before 1948, were called Statutory Rules and Orders and are still cited as, e.g., SR & O 1923 No. 752.) SIs also have short (?) titles, e.g., Medicines (Contact Lens Fluids and Other Substances) (Termination of Transitional Exemptions) Order 1981 (SI 1981 No. 1689).

SUMMARY: STATUTORY INSTRUMENT FINDING
(For more detailed researching, see Chapter 10.)

1.   You have a SI by number and want the text?

(a)   *Halsbury's SIs* Service Vol. 1 numerical index. If too recent,

(b)   its Monthly Survey index. If only summarised in this set,

(c)   QP copy in HMSO annual vol, or LEXIS. If too recent for either,

(d)   HMSO paper part as issued, or *Halsbury's SIs* publishers will supply copies to subscribers,

(e)   if not in (a) or (b), check for revocation in *Current Law Legislation Citator* index of 'SIs Affected'.

2.   You have SI by name and date and want the text?

(a)   *Halsbury's SIs* Consolidated Index alphabetical list; or,

(b)   subject volume of *Halsbury's SIs*.

3.   You have a statute and want to know of any SIs made under it?

(a)   *Current Law Legislation Citator* and continuation in latest monthly; or

(b)   *Current Law Statutes* Current Service; or

(c)   *Halsbury's Statutes, Supplement* and *Noter-Up.*

EXERCISE E: STATUTORY INSTRUMENTS FAMILIARITY

Try the following exercises in basic SI searching. They assume that you have available the SIs in both the HMSO and *Halsbury* sets, so if possible do them in a library which has both of these. When you have gained familiarity with SIs we can try some more advanced researching.

1.   What is SI 1991 No. 1381 about? What is its present status?

2.   The Access to Personal Files Act, s. 3 empowers the Secretary of State to make regulations enabling individuals to see files about them held by various bodies, and to make corrections and erasures, etc. How many sets of regulations have been made so far?

3.   In a work on property law you find a reference: Rule 301 of SR & O 1925 No. 1093. What is this? Is it in the library? See if you can find if there have been any recent cases on it.

4.   What is the date of the earliest piece of subordinate legislation that is still in force?

Chapter Six

Words and Phrases

'I would guess' said Lord Hailsham LC in his 1983 Hamlyn Lecture 'that over nine out of ten cases heard on appeal before the Court of Appeal or the House of Lords, either turn upon or involve the meaning of words contained in enactments of primary or secondary legislation.'

A very high percentage of all legal problems boil down in the end to the meaning of words. Sometimes words are imposed on you: they appear in Acts or statutory instruments, in contracts, insurance policies or wills, and seem ambiguous or uncertain through subsequent unforeseen happenings or transactions. At other times the situation is reversed: you have a blank sheet of paper on which to draft your document but need to be cautious in the choice of terms lest the law in the past may have given them meanings undesired by you.

Law graduates should know of plenty of cases in which odd words have been given odder meanings, but in law courses these usually crop up in cases where some principles of statutory interpretation or documentary construction have been applied. There are, however, a number of stages for the practising lawyer to go through before having – resignedly – to resort to the so-called rules of interpretation. The diagram 17.3 gives a suggested sequence of operations. For the present we will assume that a word or phrase has been imposed on you by a document and its meaning is uncertain. The first inquiry is as to whether the law has already defined the term used, given it an authoritative interpretation applicable to your case. How is this discoverable?

6.1   STAGES OF INQUIRY

There are four stages of inquiry to be gone through here. To be methodical we had better look at each in sequence; but really for present purposes it is the third stage (6.1.3) which mainly concerns us.

6.1.1   Does the Act, SI, document, etc., provide its own definitions?

See if there is any built-in glossary. If the expression is defined, that should end doubt. Some definitions do not end doubt, however: e.g., where they are merely inclusive, or where they allow exceptions 'where the context otherwise requires'. Even a definition section may sometimes need interpreting.

6.1.2   Might the Interpretation Act 1978 help?

This Act provides some very basic clarifications and the meanings of some frequently recurring terms in statutes: masculine includes feminine, singular is interchangeable with plural, 'land', 'month', 'financial year', 'writing', etc. Note however that strictly it is almost all applicable only to statutes and statutory material.

6.1.3   Has any other statute or case provided a relevant definition?

(See further 6.2 below.)

6.1.4   Would an ordinary dictionary help?
These are quite often produced in court to assist in establishing the accepted meaning of words on the assumption that Parliament (or the parties) had that in mind.

6.2   DEFINITION OF THE TERM IN OTHER LEGAL CONTEXTS

This is the third stage (6.1.3) above. The task for the researcher is to check what meaning, if any, has been given by the law to the specific word or phrase in the past. A law library must have several sources from which these meanings can be ascertained.

6.3   DICTIONARIES OF LEGALLY-DEFINED WORDS AND PHRASES

These very useful compilations seek to expound every word or phrase to which judicial, legislative or other recognised legal meaning has been attached. In doing so, they give detailed references, examples of usage and other helpful information. There are two works to be found in most law libraries: *Stroud's Judicial Dictionary* and *Words and Phrases Legally Defined*. Both are multi-volume sets with periodic supplements keeping them up to date. Although covering much the same ground, they differ considerably in both the words they select and in their manner of treatment. It is therefore always wise to consult both these works. Incidentally, should you ever need to use the American equivalent of these compilations, it is called *Words and Phrases*. The set contains about 90 large volumes, plus supplements.

6.4   *HALSBURY'S LAWS* VOL. 56 AND *ANNUAL ABRIDGMENT*

Following the general index to this encyclopaedia there is in Vol. 56 an index of words and phrases occurring anywhere in the main volumes. This sometimes throws up a phrase missed by the dictionaries. This is carried on for each year by the *Annual Abridgment* volumes which have a separate section of the year's words and phrases listed near to the beginning.

6.5   THE LR PINK AND RED INDEXES

The indexes to *The Law Reports* have a section of words and phrases under letter *W* in the subject-matter index. The *All England Reports* annual and cumulated indexes have a similar list.

6.6   *CURRENT LAW*

Each yearbook has a section of words and phrases as interpreted by
the courts that year. The monthly parts have a cumulative list under
W in the subject headings, so by looking at the latest monthly you
will find a list of all the present year's words.

6.7   *DAILY LAW REPORTS INDEX* KEYWORDS INDEXES

Although not strictly the same as words and phrases, you can get
useful further leads here to recent cases and those not reported
elsewhere. Moreover the editors of law reports and *Current Law* do
not single out as many cases on words as they might, so this further
source is welcome.

6.8   LEXIS

The computer can be a most efficient and comprehensive means of
researching word usage, if not necessarily for interpretation. It may
therefore be helpful to mention it here with a fuller look at LEXIS
later. As for accessing LEXIS for words, unless your word or phrase
is very unusual, merely offering it to LEXIS CASES file will throw
up far too many instances to check. You should give it as [word] w/10
of mean! or interpret! or constr! or defin! But more of this later.

6.9   APPLYING A DISCOVERED DEFINITION

Whilst you may be delighted to find your problem word defined for
you in one of these sources (or downcast – if the meaning is not to
your advantage), you must not mechanically transfer such definition
to your situation. To take an obvious example, a definition of 'child'
in a statute dealing with succession is likely to be quite irrelevant to
the meaning of 'child' in a statute about, say, employment conditions
or education. On the other hand statutes which are about the same
or related subject-matter (what lawyers call *pari materia*) have to be
read together, including their definitions. Obviously in tax, theft, and
road traffic legislation respectively, the terms 'income', 'deception'

and 'vehicle' have to be given a consistent meaning throughout. The same applies to precedents of interpretation: you must use your own judgment to see if the meaning given by the court is appropriate to your case.

6.9.1 Example

A new Act of Parliament allows compensation for disturbance in certain circumstances. However, it states that the disturbance has to be shown to be 'of significant proportion or degree'. The Act does not define or explain this phrase. You are consulted by a disturbed client. How would you advise him?

6.9.2 Analysis

The words 'proportion' and 'degree' are merely different types of extent and are not a problem. The difficulty is 'significant'. In the ordinary dictionaries this open-ended word can mean substantial, appreciable, more than negligible, or just showing signs. Has it perhaps been defined in any other statute or been construed by a court? If you look thoroughly, you will find a case about a sex shop. You will there see what an appeal court has said the word means; and then you have to decide whether that meaning could be applicable to your case.

SUMMARY: WORDS AND PHRASES
(See also diagram on in 17.3.)

1.   Are you sure it is a question of the legal meaning of a word or phrase? if so,

2.   Check to see if the document itself provides a definition, or clue, to its meaning. If none,

3.   Check both *Stroud's* and *Words and Phrases* and their supplements.

4.   If no help, then, depending on your assessment of likelihoods, check any or all of:

(a) *Halsbury's Laws*, Vol. 56 and more recent *Annual Abridgment(s)*;

(b) last year's *Current Law Yearbook* and latest monthly index of this year's words;

(c) *Law Reports* red index volume, and this year's pink index, of words and phrases;

(d) this year's *DLRI* keywords indexes;

(e) LEXIS.

5. If none of these is helpful, try an ordinary (big) dictionary.

6. If something helpful (or positively unhelpful) emerges, consider carefully its applicability.

EXERCISE F: WORDS AND PHRASES

1. Find the most recent judicial explanations of:

(a) curtilage;

(b) reasonable time;

(c) land covered with water;

(d) likely.

2. Has it been held defamatory to describe a lawyer as 'a dunce'?

3. An Act requires a notice to be 'displayed outside premises'. Is it sufficient to stick it to the inside of the window of the building so that it is visible outside but remains inside?

4. A recent will left a large legacy 'to my nephew Harold, if he returns to England'. Harold has returned from Australia, where he lives, and is claiming the legacy. He admits that he intends to go back

as soon as he has it. The executors say this is not what the testator meant. Are they right ?

5. Fred took out holiday insurance and went to Spain for two weeks. While there he sunbathed excessively, got heatstroke and died. His insurance covered him against 'accidental bodily injury caused by outward violent and visible means'. His widow is claiming under the policy. Advise the insurers if they are liable.

Chapter Seven

Noting Your Research

It is a very common experience for researchers to find things and then to forget where – and even how – they found them. Losing knowledge can be as annoying in its own way as losing material possessions. To avoid this you need to have a disciplined method of note-taking when researching. This will provide a safeguard against losses of information caused by casualness or interruptions of research, and it can also help to organise the research in a structured way. Bear in mind that the end product has to be something which you can effectively report, draft, opine upon, explain in lay terms, or otherwise impart in whatever form is called for. To do this effectively, you have to have the means of ready recall, quick grasp and comprehension of your research, perhaps after a long interval.

Just as no two students have the same approach to taking lecture notes, so no two lawyers note their researches in the same way. You will gradually develop your own method and emphasis but here are some practical guidelines.

7.1   BEFORE YOU START

Get yourself a research notebook. The most useful sort are those with holes punched, because you may need to rearrange your findings in a different order when it comes to expressing your conclusions. If you prefer to use one of the long notebooks favoured by lawyers, make sure you can remove the pages and have enough space left to punch them for permanent filing in a suitable ring-binder.

7.2 WHAT ARE YOU LOOKING FOR?

At the outset you should have a list of aims, questions to be answered or propositions of law to be established. These should a⁻ise naturally from the analysis and classification of the facts you will already have extracted.

For example, if we look back at the *Lady Frail* case with which we started, and assuming that we know nothing beyond general tort principles, we might identify a number of possible issues of law:

(a)   Are damages recoverable in principle for mere emotional injury?

(b)   If yes to (a), is mere shock or fright enough, or must there be some consequential physical illness?

(c)   In either event in (b), are damages recoverable if the shock was caused through fear merely for material objects with no fear for human life or limb?

(d)   If yes to (c), is a defence of consent to the risk to the object threatened applicable in principle to defeat the claim?

(e)   If no to (d), is a defence of contributory negligence in relation to the object threatened applicable in mitigation of the claim?

(f)   If yes to (e), with a view to advising on a settlement or payment into court, what percentage deduction would be proper in these circumstances?

Here there are six distinct – though interdependent – legal issues to be researched by anyone with no initial knowledge of liability for nervous shock. For each one we need an authoritative legal answer.

Of course it is quite common to find a case or statute which answers two or more of the initial questions. Nevertheless it is important to remember that in unfocused problems we are researching legal issues, not cases or statutes. Therefore it is good practice to write down each issue in the form of a question as the heading of a fresh page of your notebook. Use the rest of the page (and continuation if necessary) for your findings applicable just to that heading. In this way your research will be issue-led, and information will accumulate in a semi-organised pre-selected way. You may have to apply the same authority to more than one heading and conversely you may have to head up a further sheet if a new, more subtle sub-issue emerges.

7.3   WHERE AND WHEN ARE YOU DOING IT?

Note the date, place (which library) and time your research commences, and note this afresh whenever you are interrupted and recommence. (This information may be wanted anyway if your research time is chargeable.)

7.4   WHICH SOURCES ARE YOU USING?

Note where and in which sources you began (e.g., *Halsbury's Laws* index – nervous shock = Vol. 34,8). Note each new starting point in this way before you have even gone to get it from the shelf. Do not assume you will remember how you found it. Lay a trail so that you can always retrace your steps.

7.5   WHAT HAVE YOU FOUND?

Each authority, statute, case, etc., that you are referred to should be listed by you. Then check them in turn for relevance. Tick each one when you have read it to remind yourself you have done so, and then cross your tick to indicate that it was not on the point sought. Against each helpful or contrary authority's reference, give a very brief summary of the significant part: one sentence, or catchwords, of a case; the vital words of a section or SI. Note page and line, or section, paragraph or other number of any vital passage. The same applies to useful or unwelcome statements or quotations.

7.6 WHAT DO YOU THINK?

Add a brief note to the ticked authorities showing your provisional reaction or opinion, e.g.:

— note the definition is inclusionary, not exhaustive,

— arguably *obiter*,

— must argue for literal interpretation,

— could be *ultra vires?*,

— persuasive authority only, but would be followed, etc.

These instant reactions may be hasty and need revision, but you will find them a helpful reminder, sparing the need to reread and reassess after an interval. They will also help you to marshal your arguments for their ultimate presentation and if it is later suggested that there is an error or omission in your conclusions, you will be able to recheck your reasoning process at each stage.

7.7 AFTER YOU HAVE FINISHED

Preserve your researches. You may need to reorganise your separate sheets of issues into a different order from the original sequence. Some may have ceased to be issues at all. After you have written up or communicated your findings as required, do not discard your research notes. If they are punched they can be filed in a logical order in a ring-file. It will help to identify them quickly later if you mark or group the pages in some way to separate each piece of research from the next. Transparent plastic punched pockets are excellent for this purpose.

Remember that it may be quite some time – years, even – before your advice or report comes to be tested. You should not be put in the position of desperately trying to recall why you came to that conclusion, where you found that information or whether you checked some unmentioned authorities.

In addition, it is not uncommon for new problems to ring bells from times long past. If this happens, it is very helpful – and impressive – to be able to have instant recall of chapter and verse (but do not overlook the need to update).

SUMMARY: NOTING YOUR RESEARCH

1. Keep a notebook for all research and a storage file.

2. State each issue on a fresh page.

3. Note date and time of each beginning.

4. Note:

    (a)   each stage of search;

    (b)   each authority checked and rejected;

    (c)   relevant authorities' precise citations; and

    (d)   relevant authorities' essential points.

5. Add comments to relevant authorities.

6. Reorganise your pages into logical sequence.

7. File and keep.

Chapter Eight

More Advanced Problem Solving

So far we have looked at the rudiments of law finding and then tried applying these to some basic legal sources. We have to get deeper into these and further sources but first we need to consider in more depth the technique of problem solving. There are a number of general principles which the lawyer has to keep in mind throughout researching.

8.1 CHOOSING THE 'RIGHT WAY'

Mostly there is not one. There is no one correct method to research in law. Almost always there will be two or more alternative routes to the same destination. Some may be quicker, offering short cuts; others covering more ground more thoroughly. Most lawyers, with practice and experience, evolve their own preferred route, depending on their area of practice and sources to hand. The beginner should ideally explore all the main routes so as to understand their alternative merits. In that sense there *is* one right way.

8.2 LAST THINGS FIRST

Your object is to arrive at a reliable, realistic, practical and client-oriented conclusion of law as applicable to the essential facts correctly extracted. A learned overview of the law, such as might have gained high marks for the LLB student, is not wanted. If you bear this in mind, it will help to keep your feet on the ground and prevent your research pulling you in all directions. You have to be resourceful but not perfectionist.

8.3   RESEARCH MUST BE IMPARTIAL

Of course your object is to serve your client's case or needs, but it is no service to select the authorities which suit you and to ignore those which do not. Once you have found the relevant law see if there is any way of avoiding or minimising any disadvantageous implications it may have. Do not however, dismiss them.

8.4   FINDING THE 'RIGHT' ANSWER

All the problems set in the exercises in this book have more or less 'correct' and ascertainable solutions. This is necessary, or at any rate, desirable, for learning purposes. However, it does give a slightly false picture of the law in practice, where there is sometimes no such clear-cut answer, and sometimes no ascertainable law at all.

8.5   FINDING NOTHING

It follows from the preceding point that in real life, finding nothing, no case on the point, no legislation, nothing written about it, is not necessarily failure. Always provided you have done your researches thoroughly, it is success. If there is really no authority directly in point, you are free to construct what arguments or analogies you can. However, your instinct should tell you when and where there is likely to be some relevant law on the point, and should prompt you to search more widely or thoroughly or analogously before accepting a nil finding.

8.6   PREMATURE REFINEMENT

One common cause of the law researcher finding nothing is pre-selecting or over-refining the field researched too early. For example, a landlord and tenant or matrimonial law query might be covered completely by a statutory provision. If you make up your mind that it is a matter of case law, you may eventually find your way into the statute by the back door, or you may miss it entirely. Likewise you may go straight to the SIs index for something which, being minute and technical, seems the right place to look whereas it could be in a statute schedule. If you are not sure in what form of law the answer, if any, is to be found, keep your options open by starting your research at the general level until you have got your first leads.

8.7 PROBING THE PROBLEM

In everyday practice a typical unfocused problem may start out as a mass of undigested facts. Some will seem important, others peripheral, while still others may be missing altogether. From all of these the lawyer has to select what appear to be the vital matters and then from these to identify the legal issues. As most lawyers tend to specialise to some extent, they do not often find they have to venture into totally unknown territory. But even the most seasoned practitioner will occasionally come up against a new problem area and the beginner certainly will when almost everything is new.

How, then, does the experienced lawyer go about extracting the questions from the raw material? As a matter of second nature and probably quite unconsciously, by probing the facts and, if necessary, the client for further facts.

There is of course some circularity in this process. Experienced lawyers are able to select and reject facts as significant or non-significant because they already know the ways of the law. But this is where your legal training begins to show. You know more than perhaps you realise, about the general organisation and classification, criteria and distinctions of the law. Your sense of legal relevance, whilst perhaps not yet assured, is already well ahead of the intelligent layman's and it will improve with every exercise.

To demonstrate the point, let us have some further exercises, in out-of-the-way areas of law.

EXERCISE G

1. Peter, Paul and Mary want to go carol singing for charity on
Christmas Day. They intend to stand outside Victoria station. They
have trained their dog to carry one of their collecting boxes. Have
you any legal advice to offer them?

Analysis: This type of 'can I do this?' legal inquiry can be very
difficult because it may require the lawyer to run through a range of
possible legal implications, calling not just for knowledge but legal
imagination; and the more so when what is proposed is seemingly
innocuous.

However, whether the facts are complicated or, as in this case,
deceptively simple, the technique is the same: probe the problem, test
every fact for significance: who is involved? is that important? what
is involved? type of property, amount, legal service desired, remedy
sought, where? when? Each time consider if there could be any legal
significance in the answer.

To elaborate, the facts of a problem may disclose categories to which
the law attaches special significance. For example, are any of the
following elements present? If they are, could that be positively or
negatively significant? You know enough to recognise what further
considerations some of the following might import:

(a) Parties: private individuals? public company? government
department? local authority? bank? trade union? trespasser? trustee?
bankrupt? agent? spouses? child?

(b) Subject-matter: type of property/activity/relationship? inven-
tion? vehicle? animal? right of way? misleading statement? will?
lease? insurance policy? shares? ship? personal injury? goodwill?
know-how?

(c) Place: the highway? aboard ship? abroad? hospital? school?
farm?

(d) Time: night? Sunday? years ago? after/before a legally
significant date?

(e) Result wanted/opposed: compensation? specific remedy? judicial review? patent? licence? flotation? winding up? disqualification? extradition? security for costs? admissibility of evidence? quashing of conviction?

Applying these probings to the rather sparse facts of the problem,

(a) Who are Peter, Paul and Mary? Are they children or adults, and is that important? Is the participation of a dog relevant?

(b) What are they proposing to do? Sing and collect money for charity. Might the law have something to say about either? Why should it?

(c) Where will they be doing it? In a public place. Could that be the subject of some regulation?

(d) When will they be doing it? Is there anything special about the date?

Needless to say, there is some quite clear (though surprising) law applicable to these facts. Some of the questions posed will point you in the right direction, whilst others are false starts. The keyword approach will work here if you answer the questions very fully, but you must think of plenty of alternative expressions: charity, singing, song, music, collection, collecting box, money, public place, station, street, dog, animal, Christmas, etc. For example, you know that 'charity' is very much a key concept in our law, yet it is not an operative word here. Whereas the real keywords as recognised by the law are hardly expressed in the given facts and only emerge if we paraphrase persistently. However, we have done enough to try our various alternatives in *Halsbury's Laws*. Try your luck with it and then try the two following problems.

2. The City Council is equally divided between Conservative and Labour members. The Mayor, who presides, is a Labour member. Whenever the Council votes on a politically loaded matter the result is a tie. So the Mayor, who has voted already with the Labour side, then purports to vote for that side again, tipping the balance. The Conservatives say he has no right to do this and are seeking to challenge him in the courts. Will they succeed?

3. The bulk carrier *Tubig*, proceeding under compulsory pilotage, collided with a dredger. The dredger owners are suing the *Tubig* owners alleging negligent navigation. The *Tubig* owners say that if (which is not admitted) their ship was negligently navigated, it was the fault of the pilot for which they cannot be held liable. Alternatively, if they are liable to the dredger owners, they can join the harbour authority as a third party, because it is the employer of the pilot and therefore vicariously liable for any negligence by him. Advise the *Tubig* owners if they are correct.

8.8 SOME COMMON HINDRANCES TO LAW FINDING

8.8.1 Arbitrary classifications

It will seem a little unfair, when you have analysed and correctly classified your raw material, to be frustrated by the inconsistent terminology of categories with which the law abounds. The trouble is that different law publishers may use differing subject labels for the same legal concepts. One gets over this in the first place by trial and error. For matrimonial matters, for example, you may have to try under 'husband and wife', 'family law', 'domestic relations', 'divorce', 'matrimonial property', 'spouses', 'marriage' or any new sub-classification which may be invented. Similarly with what used to be 'master and servant' and has become 'employment law', 'labour law', 'industrial law', and given rise to 'trade union law', 'equal opportunities', 'redundancy payments' and so forth. Of course a good index should cross-refer you, but they do not always do so.

8.8.2 Misleading keywords

Often keywords obligingly present themselves in the facts fully kitted-out in their legal garb: will, loan, party-wall, etc. Sometimes however, a client uses lay terms which have to be translated into legalities; he may say 'pavement', 'rent', or 'embezzlement' when what we say is 'highway', 'mesne profits' and 'theft' respectively. Sometimes, conversely, a client may use legal terms inappropriately providing you with misleading keywords: 'nuisance phone calls', 'guaranteed goods', 'my premises were robbed last night'. You then have to retranslate such pseudo-legal usages back to their correct designation.

8.8.3 Totally concealed keywords

Occasionally you will be faced with a problem where the key to unlock the law is totally missing. Once you are familiar with the particular area of law and know all its terms of art, you should have no difficulty. Until then and in the absence of help from colleagues, you will just have to try and penetrate the subject area to see how it labels itself. Below are two examples of problems where the keyword is absent and unguessable. Try your hand with them and do not be discouraged if you draw blank. The answers are on pages 132–3.

Ultimately all these hindrances are surmounted in the same way; by paraphrasing, thinking of synonyms, scanning the indexes, finding alternative ways of expressing or classifying concepts. It comes with experience, and quite quickly. Meanwhile if you are at a loss and cannot get help, the *Halsbury's Laws* index remains your best hope.

EXERCISE H: CONCEALED KEYWORDS

1. Henry, the owner of a newly-converted house, wants to let rooms on weekly terms. He wants to avoid giving any sort of security of tenure or rent protection. Henry has heard that if he provides coffee and tea for his tenants, they will be outside any of the legislation. He therefore proposes to put a hot drinks machine in the basement room which has kitchen facilities, so that occupants can help themselves to free drinks each morning and evening, and thus will not be regarded as tenants. Will he succeed?

2. Oscar, a chiropractor, has been told by the Customs and Excise that he has to add VAT to his charges to patients. Oscar says that he has always understood that there is an EC Directive which requires the medical and related professions to be exempted from having to charge VAT. He asks you to advise with a view to appealing to the VAT Tribunal.

Chapter Nine

Articles, Case Notes, Statute Notes: Researching the Journals

Practitioners' libraries may have some periodicals you will recognise from your academic studies but the emphasis of their holdings will be on practitioners' specialised periodicals. In every specialised area of legal practice there are now legal or professional journals which you will want to scan if those areas are of concern to you. More generally, the weeklies (NLJ, SJ, LSG) keep up a running commentary on all current and pending legal happenings, professional news and opinion. A browse through one of these each week must now become a habit for you in order to be well informed.

However, even within these limits it is difficult to keep up with the range of periodical literature now currently offered to lawyers. When it comes to research we need help in finding what has been written on any given development or topic, case or statute, by legal experts in the recent or more distant past. Apart from citations in the footnotes of textbooks there are several tools for opening up this legal literature exactly where we want.

9.1 *CURRENT LAW* AND *CURRENT LAW YEARBOOK*

The usefulness of these in listing current books and periodical articles was mentioned earlier. But they put them only under broad subject headings, and only substantial articles are included. The same is true of *Halsbury's Laws* which in their *Monthly Survey* booklets and *Annual Abridgments* have a similar listing. These selections may suffice for many purposes. However, we now have a more comprehensive and speedy way of accessing recent legal writing:

9.2 *LEGAL JOURNALS INDEX*

This started in 1986. It lists every article in a very wide range of UK legal periodicals (some of them only quasi-legal) by title, by subject-matter, and by author's name; and where it is a case note or statute note, by the case or statute name. It comes out promptly in monthly parts and is cumulated quarterly and annually. It is also available on-line.

LJI is a most useful new tool for research into recent developments. It can be valuable both as your first port of call before venturing into the unknown as well as your final checkpoint, when you think you have the answer from primary sources.

When you are faced with a complex new piece of legislation (whether from Westminster, Whitehall or Brussels) or a recent case whose meaning or implications are hard to grasp, it is very likely that some clever commentator will have written about it in some periodical or other. LJI enables you to find any such article, however brief and in however esoteric a journal. Remember that a controversial new piece of legislation may have attracted a good deal of professional comment during its passage through Parliament and, similarly, an appellate court decision while on its way up. All such comment should be accessible through LJI.

Occasionally a significant or controversial point gets its first airing in a book review. Or we may feel the need for a book with fuller and more systematic guidance than any short article can present. LJI therefore very helpfully lists reviews of law books. With so many published nowadays, we need this help to know what to read and buy, as well as to see what one expert thinks of another's ideas in what may be a new area of law.

Have a browse through LJI, and see how easy it is to find known and unknown articles. Note also at the front its list of initials of every journal referred to, and its listing of publishers of these with their addresses. Finally note that if your library subscribes to LJI, its publishers will supply a copy of any article listed, by post or by FAX.

9.3 INDEX TO LEGAL PERIODICALS

Some larger libraries have this serial. It is an American publication and its emphasis is therefore on American journals but it does also list articles in some of the major British and Commonwealth journals. It appears in monthly parts which are cumulated quarterly and annually. Titles and authors are indexed together. Articles on cases (mostly US cases) are indexed separately. It is a useful source for comparative Anglo-American research, and for international and of course US legal developments and thinking; and for going back to before 1986 when LJI started. (For wider comparative research academic libraries may have another American publication *Index to Foreign Legal Periodicals*, also covering non-common-law writings in English, and foreign legal writing generally.)

9.4 'CURRENT LAW INDEX'

This is another American monthly. Its title is confusing since:

(a) it has nothing to do with our own home-grown *Current Law* service, and

(b) it is not about current law but about current legal writing.

These reservations apart, this is an excellent newcomer among contemporary research tools. For historical research it cannot replace *Index to Legal Periodicals* which has been going for most of the century but the coverage is a little wider, and still growing; it is well indexed and easy to use. It is cumulated quarterly and annually.

9.5   JOURNALS ON LEXIS

The database of LEXIS includes a UKJNL library. This offers the text of every article in the *New Law Journal* and *Law Society's Gazette* since 1986, and now also has those in the *Estates Gazette*. Since almost every significant legal and professional happening is written about in these periodicals, and at about the time it occurs, this can be a valuable source of contemporary comment on the legal scene. It is especially useful where a change in the law is in contemplation or mere speculation, so that the possible impact on existing law is discussed. You select the ALLJNL file and then search in the same way as for case or statute law, trying suitable words and connectors. The special virtue of this library is in updating, so more will be said about this in Chapter 16.

SUMMARY: LOOKING FOR LEGAL WRITING

1.   Searching for discussion of developments, cases, statutes, regulations, etc., affecting English law?

(a)   recent? LJI appropriate indexes;

(b)   pre-1986? CLYB.

2.   Looking for legal writing in non-English, or not specifically English, areas?

(a)   LJI; then –

(b)   *Index to Legal Periodicals* or '*Current Law Index*'.

3.   Looking for writings of specific author?

(a)   LJI author/book review indexes;

(b)   *Index to Legal Periodicals* or '*Current Law Index*' author index.

4.   You have researched a case, Act, regulation, committee report, etc., and think you have found what you were looking for – if recent, you could still get a further slant on it by reading current opinion in journal articles cited in LJI.

EXERCISE I: UK JOURNALS

1.   Find an article in 1988 about pupillage in chambers being more like unpaid labour than education.

2.   Find the most recent article you can on:

   (a)   Romalpa clauses;

   (b)   Dogs Act 1871;

   (c)   the disposal of dead fetuses.

3.   How many articles has the firm of Allen & Overy had published so far this year?

4.   Has the recent unreported Californian case of *Lewis Galoob Toys* v *Nintendo* been noted in any UK journal?

5.   Find an article to help you understand the Price Marking Order 1991.

Chapter Ten

Statutory Instruments – Researching and Updating

We looked briefly at statutory instruments earlier, as they appear on the library shelf. Accessing and updating them is complicated. Remember they are now all contained on the STATIS file of LEXIS.

Assuming that you have done your basic research and are fairly confident that it is a SI that you want, the following notes will help you.

10.1 WHY MIGHT YOU BE LOOKING FOR A SI?

(a) Because you have an Act which is to commence on an appointed day, and you want to see whether there has been a commencement order, and, if so, what it says.

If that is all you want, do not bother to look for the SI (if any). Instead:

(i)   check *Is It In Force?* and follow through as explained previously (3.4.4.1);

(ii)   alternatively, commencement and appointed day orders are listed in the first loose-leaf volume of *Halsbury's Statutory*

Instruments, updated by the *Monthly Survey* section in the same binder; and in the latest monthly part of *Current Law*;

(iii)   from 1992, the text of commencement orders is set out in the service file of *Current Law Statutes*;

(iv)   if no order appears in any of these, update by checking in the last few weeks' issues of one of the legal weeklies: NLJ, LSG or SJ.

(b)   Because you have a section of an Act which says 'regulations may be made under this section . . .' or words to that effect, and you want to know if there have been any.

You can find out in various ways:

(i)   the annotations to that section in *Halsbury's Statutes,* following through into the *Cumulative Supplement* and *Noter-Up*;

(ii)   *Current Law Legislation Citator* and latest monthly *Cumulative Citator*;

(iii)   *Halsbury's Statutory Instruments* table of statutes indexes all enabling Acts with their implementation;

(iv)   *Index to Government Orders* and its monthly supplement, published by HMSO,

followed in all cases by a scan of the last few issues of one of the legal weeklies, and then the HMSO daily list.

(c)   Because you have been referred to a SI by its number.

(i)   *Halsbury's Statutory Instruments* chronological list in the first loose-leaf volume, will tell you in which main volume the SI is located. If the SI is more recent than the last one shown, check the *Monthly Survey* key;

(ii)   alternatively, the blue HMSO volumes have their year and numbers on their spine.

(d)   Because you have the name of a SI but not its number, e.g., the Road Vehicles (Construction and Use) Regulations of uncertain date.

Until recently there was no comprehensive index of all SI short titles. *Halsbury's Laws Annual Abridgments* have listed each year's SIs alphabetically since these volumes began in 1974. CLYB has done the same since 1984. So if you know the year or approximate year, you can still get the SI number and also a summary of its content this way. However, the *Consolidated Index* volume to *Halsbury's Statutory Instruments* now has an alphabetical index of all short-titled SIs issued to the end of last year. Of course if it may have been issued in the present year, check *Current Law* latest monthly part's index of SIs. If not there, it sounds as if you may have the name wrong. So try to classify the subject-matter and then find it in the title key in the first loose-leaf volume of *Halsbury's Statutory Instruments*; or if that does not work, search in the *Consolidated Index* by trying suitable keywords.

(e)   Because your problem seems to be in a typical SI area of technical law, but you do not know if there is any actual SI applicable.

This is not a very likely point of entry and you should do more preparatory research before plunging in. You could try the *Consolidated Index*, or the current *Index to Government Orders* (the official two-volume index by subject-matter). But it would be more methodical to go first to the appropriate practitioners' textbook, or back to *Halsbury's Laws* index and follow through.

(f)   You have the SI but do not know if it is still effective.

In *Current Law Legislation* Citator there is a list of every SI which has been in any way affected (amended, revoked, etc.) during the period 1947–91. Follow through by looking in the subject index to the latest monthly part of *Current Law* for more recent and pending happenings.

(g)   You have the SI but do not know if it has been considered in any cases.

(i)   the *Law Reports* pink (and if necessary red) index lists SIs considered. However, even though these cover many series of reports, they may still omit cases on SIs because of the highly specialised areas of activity that may be involved. So –

(ii)   check in any loose-leaf specialised text book in this area, or in any appropriate specialised series of reports which has a running index;

(iii)   DLRI legislation index includes litigated SIs by name, if reported in the dailies;

(iv)   LEXIS CASES file can be searched by SI number, name or keywords;

(v)   LEXIS ALLJNL file may reveal discussion of the SI and any litigation on it.

(h)   You are looking for what is a SI in origin, but is better known in another form.

The best examples are the various courts' rules: Supreme Court, County Court, Crown Court, Magistrates' Courts, etc. These are of course more conveniently found in the White and Green books, *Stone's* etc. But for any very recent amendment to the rules, not yet in the particular practice book's supplement, you may need to go to the HMSO Queen's Printer's issue. *Halsbury's Statutory Instruments* monthly supplement should at least summarise the amendment, but may not print it in full.

That reminds us to repeat that if we need the text of a recent SI urgently and it is only summarised in *Halsbury's SIs* (and LEXIS has not got it yet), the *Halsbury Statutory Instruments* publishers will supply copies to subscribers as part of their service.

EXERCISE J: STATUTORY INSTRUMENT RESEARCHING

1.   Clarissa saw an advert for a slimming aid which claimed to be 'totally new' and 'absolutely safe' and whose users were 'guaranteed

to lose weight'. She spent a lot of money on it and used it as directed but it had no effect. She wonders if she has any legal redress.

Analysis: Your existing legal knowledge might suggest breach of contract, a kind of carbolic smoke-ball case. But what is her real complaint? That it is not new? That it is not safe? The claim for newness has little relevance to her grievance; and she has suffered no harmful effects suggesting lack of safety. So her real complaint is of ineffectiveness, which is not a very promising basis for a civil action. Some lateral thinking here might help. See if you can discern another keyword among the facts which could give her an alternative way of proceeding, and then research along that line.

2.   Food manufacturing company have been making and selling tomato ketchup for some years to their own special formula. The local food standards authority now say that they have received a complaint that the ketchup contains hardly any tomato and that this is disguised by various other vegetables and flavourings. Does tomato ketchup have to contain any tomato? If so, how much? May it contain any other vegetable substances?

3.   Uplift, while travelling by hovercraft across the Channel, was injured in an accident caused by the negligent navigation of the craft. Also some of his luggage was damaged. What is the maximum Uplift can claim for his injuries and loss?

4.   Mary recently bought contact lenses. One is fine but the other is very uncomfortable. She went back to see the optician who tested her eyes and fitted the lenses but found that there was a new optician working there who told her that the man she had seen had left the practice and emigrated. The new optician, who was very busy seeing patients, told her she should persevere with the lenses and she would get used to them. Mary is very dissatisfied and no longer able to wear them. Apart from contract, has she any legal redress?

5.   What is the daily maximum fine for breach of the Insolvency Act 1986, s. 109(2)?

6.   After an evening out, Reg drove his girlfriend Gloria home. They parked outside her house talking in the car. As it was a cold

night, Reg kept the engine running, revving it from time to time. Pc Killjoy was pushing his bicycle along the pavement approaching the parked car from the rear. As he drew level with the car, Gloria opened the front passenger door to get out. The door struck the Pc's bicycle but he managed to take evasive action and no damage was done. Killjoy told Gloria that she would be prosecuted for not looking before opening the door. He also told Reg that he would be reported with a view to prosecution for keeping his engine running. Reg and Gloria say they have never heard of any such offences and ask you to advise them.

7.   If you want to go into outer space, what legal requirement must you satisfy and how much will this cost? Whom do you apply to?

8.   What is the maximum amount of capital that may be raised through the business expansion scheme by the issue of eligible shares?

9.   Which professional bodies' dealings has the Legal Services Ombudsman been given authority to investigate?

10.   A woman pushing a pram was about to cross the road on a zebra crossing. The pram was on the crossing but the woman herself was still on the pavement. A motorist drove past in front of the pram without stopping. Did he commit an offence?

Chapter Eleven

Widening Case Law Researches

11.1 *THE DIGEST*

We saw earlier that *The Digest* is a multi-volume treasure house of summaries of reported cases. It might have been more illuminating if its publishers had given it the family name, something like *Halsbury's Encyclopaedia of Case Law*, for that is what it really is. The number of cases it contains must now be approaching the half-million mark. They are drawn from England, Scotland, Ireland, and the Commonwealth: in other words from the whole English-speaking world outside the USA. To this is now added the case law of the EC and European human rights cases.

The Digest therefore gives us access to a vast range of case law going back in time and sideways in jurisdiction, far beyond the holdings of any normal law library. Like its *Halsbury* stable-mates, its contents are arranged alphabetically under headings in its 50-odd main volumes, plus indexes, continuation volumes and supplements.

11.2 WHEN *THE DIGEST* IS APPROPRIATE

On any occasion when you are thinking of researching in *The Digest* you should first ask yourself if it is appropriate to do so. A newcomer to English law, on seeing *Digest* volumes titled on their spine

'Companies' or 'Value Added Tax' or 'Patents and Inventions' might think that this is a good place to start solving problems in these areas. But you know better than that: that the general law in these areas is in statutes and regulations to which one must go first. On the other hand, looking along the spines of the volumes, one sees titles of subject areas which are still substantially case based: Libel and Slander, Landlord and Tenant, Evidence, Estoppel, Bailment, and so on. (There is even a title 'Custom and Usages'.) Even in these areas, however, think carefully and do not resort to *The Digest* until your research has reached a point where you can say with confidence that it is purely instances of case law that you need to discover. Remember also the related point which we made earlier on our first acquaintance. A reported case remains a reported case, or so *The Digest* appears to think, notwithstanding that what it decided has been completely overthrown by later statutes; and moreover the digest of the case will not tell you this has happened. So think both before and after you use it.

11.3   ACCESSING *THE DIGEST*

11.3.1   Subject-matter searching

(a)   The *Consolidated Index* keys into all the headings and sub-headings in the set. It does not unfortunately key directly into the cases themselves, their facts and other details in the way that, for example, *Halsbury's Laws* is indexed. Nevertheless it can still be a useful starting point. If your problem is about, say, liability for pollution, the index will send you to the *Public Health* volume but it also suggests that you might want to check under Nuisance and under Shipping in the index. However, if you are having to go to this index to find the appropriate heading, it could be that you have not yet correctly identified your question as residing in case law. After all, there is plenty of legislation on pollution. Should you be starting with a case search? Go back and reconsider 11.2.1 above and think whether a standard textbook or the general index to *Halsbury's Laws* might be a better starting point.

(b)   Suppose however, you want to explore the reported case law on a recognised legal category and it really is case law, e.g., nuisance caused by trees in the neighbouring premises. Since you know that this sort of interference may constitute nuisance, and that private nuisance concepts are still mostly common law, you could go straight to the volume with Nuisance on the spine, 36(2). At the beginning of the Nuisance section there is a table of contents setting out the headings under which this title is organised. Search these systematically and find the page applicable.

(c)   Note that each case name and reference is given at the end of digest of facts and decision. Then, following that, you get any subsequent English cases in which it was cited to any real effect, and what that effect was ('apprvd', 'distd', etc.). (This incidentally is a useful alternative source to *Current Law Case Citator* for checking the subsequent history of a case, and is wider, covering the whole of that history, not just the 1947-to-date citations.)

(d)   Note further that after that there are printed in smaller type any related cases from other jurisdictions.

(e)   Pursue any cross-references given which look helpful.

(f)   Always remember that your research is not finished until you have followed through, using the apparatus provided for this by *The Digest*. See below.

11.3.2   Chasing up specific cases

You have a case by name but its reference is to some remote, obscure or unrecognisable reports, or you have a case name with no reference. The four-volume index of cases gives every case in *The Digest* and your case is most likely to be there. The index does not refer you directly to the case, but to the volume by number and title. There you will find the volume's own case index, giving the paragraph number.

Note that the main case index to *The Digest* in some ways includes more than the *Current Law Case Citator* or even the *Halsbury's Laws* case index. Note also how *The Digest* index is itself updated annually: see below.

11.3.3   Following through

(a)   After a subject-matter search: *The Digest* has a cumulative supplement, issued annually. Like the rest of the *Halsbury* family, it has a noter-up section which provides additions and revisions to case digests in the main volumes. Having therefore found your cases of relevance, always check in the supplement, under the same headings and paragraph numbers, for the past year's developments. You may find nothing; or new case law digested; or you may be referred to a named case in one of the *Continuation Volumes* of *The Digest*, into which new cases are off-loaded to save the annual supplement becoming too bulky.

(b)   After a named-case search: the *Cumulative Supplement* also has a case index with references to all the cases contained in the supplement itself. If under 11.3.2 above you failed to find your named case, it could be more recent and therefore listed here. If you did find it, note the paragraph number and check for later references to the case in the supplement.

(c)   Further updating: the supplement is only annual, so you should still check for the latest English cases, if they are relevant to your search, in *Current Law* and DLRI as described earlier.

11.4   GENERAL KEY TO *THE DIGEST*

This is also located in the supplement volume. You will find all the very many series of law reports specified with their cryptic initials. All the later case effects ('distd', 'approvd' etc.) are explained (did you know the nuances of difference between 'applied', 'approved' and 'followed', for example?). And a section on 'How to use *The Digest*' is a useful refresher.

SUMMARY: USING *THE DIGEST*

1.   Be sure it is case law and only case law you need.

2.   For subject-matter, select by spine title and list of contents. If in doubt, search *Consolidated Index*.

3.   For specific cases search case index.

4.   Complete each search by checking *Supplement*.

EXERCISE K: USING *THE DIGEST*

1.   Find an English case on whether the proprietor of a wine bar can insist that only men can stand at the bar while women have to drink at tables.

2.   Find a case from Canada on a patient in hospital being burned by a hot water bottle.

3.   Find the most recent case in *The Digest* on an occupier's duty to trespassers.

4.   Find a case from Australia on whether the ringing of church bells on a Sunday morning could be an actionable nuisance.

5.   Find a case involving Switzerland which says that a corporation has no right to freedom of conscience or religion.

6.   Which, according to *The Digest*, is the most recent case to consider *Street* v *Mountford*?

Chapter Twelve

Forms and Precedents

A good deal of a lawyer's time is taken up with the creation of formal documents: conveyances and contracts, pleadings and opinions, even statutes and regulations. These usually have to be in conformity with required or approved existing patterns and styles. You will already have learned something of the rudiments of drafting, and also studied cases in which bad drafting has led to costly litigation.

The difference between forms and precedents is that forms are documents imposing a prescribed framework into which we have to fit our individual content as precisely dictated, whereas with precedents, we start with a blank sheet of paper and theoretically a free hand, only to find that we have to conform with some well-worn way of drafting.

12.1 BOOKS OF STANDARD PRECEDENTS

Collections of precedents are among the oldest literature of the law going back to the Middle Ages. In law libraries today there are three main sorts:

(a) Collections specific to a particular area of practice, e.g., *Bullen and Leake* on pleadings; Longman's *Practical Commercial Precedents*; and so forth.

(b)   Specialised journals offering their subscribers suggested precedents to meet new situations, legal developments, e.g., *The Conveyancer*.

(c)   General multi-volume works covering the whole range of practice. In this category come the *Encyclopaedia of Forms and Precedents* and *Atkin's Court Forms*.

12.1.1   Sources of first resort

After a short time in practice lawyers who have to repeatedly draft the same classes of document tend to prefer a particular precedent book for their purposes. This may be in any of these categories. Additionally, many firms build up their own in-house collections based on shared past experience.

12.2   THE TWO GENERAL COLLECTIONS

The best thing for beginners is to get to know the multi-volume sets and their contents generally. These two sets are not only collections of forms and precedents but also important sources of associated background information. They have an organisation with which we are now familiar: main volumes in alphabetical subject order, cumulative supplements, current service, annually revised indexes, etc. What is very useful is that each title, written by a specialist editor, before giving any actual precedents offers a résumé of all the applicable law and authorities and sometimes some practical guidance as well: a sort of mini textbook, directing the reader towards the precedents which follow or the form which has to be used.

12.2.1   Allocation of contents

The *Encyclopaedia of Forms and Precedents* covers all the non-litigious areas. *Atkin's* does the corresponding job for litigious matters generally and not just court forms as its name suggests. The division of content between the two sets is far from predictable, however. Suppose, for example, you have two clients: one, nurserymen, want you to apply for legal protection for a blue tulip they have developed. The others, bookmakers, want you to get them permission to open betting shops. You will find that the necessary procedures and documentation, etc., for both of these are fully dealt with in these two sets, but the one is only in *Atkin* and the other only in the *Encyclopaedia*. Use the indexes to each to see which is where and then see if you can fathom why the publishers have put them where they are.

The obvious lesson is that if you draw a blank in your search for a precedent or form in what you think is the appropriate set, try the other one. As with all the multi-volume sets, remember to follow through to ensure your information is right up to date.

EXERCISE L: FORMS AND PRECEDENTS

1.   A TV film production company is making a film which is to include a nude scene involving an actor and actress. What should their contracts say about this? Can the actors object to the company's use of unused material in the scene, or of stills?

2.   Find the correct form of application for permission to dig up and remove a dead body from a grave. How much is the fee?

3.   Mrs T lives in a small cul-de-sac. She would like to have it closed off completely, making it into a private road. All the other householders agree. To whom and how does she apply? Should any documents or details accompany her request? Who finally decides if the road is to be closed or not?

Chapter Thirteen

Keeping Up To Date

The importance of getting up to date has been mentioned several times in connection with specific sources. We must now look at the vital process of keeping up to date in its own right, and the resources for doing it. In doing so we can repeat some of the points made earlier, hoping this is a desirable reminder.

13.1 LAWYERS' WEEKLIES

Every week of the year there are various publications which keep lawyers in touch with current and pending legal developments and professional opinion and happenings. The three most general of these are the *New Law Journal*, the *Solicitors' Journal* and the *Law Society's Gazette*. It is on these that most lawyers rely to be alerted to changes and their significance, so get into the good habit of reading at least one of these each week. If, additionally, you have the good fortune to be in a firm which produces its own in-house periodical circular of current legal intelligence, take full advantage of that. For one thing, it is likely to be even more up to date, and more relevant to your areas of practice.

It is a common experience to need to know something very specific and to have a vague recollection of reading something about it recently in some news-sheet or other. So if you can access these ephemeral sources systematically it makes them much more valuable than mere browsing material. The published weeklies are indexed at least annually, and are also searchable through LEXIS (see Chapter 16). In-house bulletins are often indexed by the librarians.

13.2 UPDATING AS A DISCIPLINE

Reading the weeklies helps in a general way to keep up to date, revising or footnoting law which you already know. But with specific researching, you should as a matter of routine procedure follow through at the end – or rather what you thought was the end – of every piece of information gleaned. If there is a supplement and current service postscripting the source you have used, use it. Remember that finding nothing when you are following through is usually welcome news. It means that what you have found is still extant law, the last word, unamended, not overruled, not yet interpreted. Conversely, if you do find something new in following through, it may set you off in a new direction of research, e.g., a new statute, line of cases or professional opinion which has to be studied afresh.

In addition to following through within a multi-volume serviced work, there are independent updating serials in the library which should always be checked as well. Let us look at three of the most useful ones, and then more closely at the nature of legal change which makes updating a necessity.

13.3 THE *CURRENT LAW* SERVICE

13.3.1 The monthly parts

We looked briefly at these earlier in 2.4.1. A fuller look at these is now necessary. The blue booklets should be kept together, in sequence, in a binder or box. This will at times have to hold up to 15 or more parts. Each monthly part sets out under alphabetical subject headings all the law of every sort and source which has happened during that month: legislation and cases, EC legal documents and cases, committee reports, law books and legal articles, etc. The subject headings are inevitably a bit arbitrary, so if you cannot find what you are looking for under the head (if any) which you chose, try some alternative classifications. You will find all the established subject headings listed at the front of each part.

If you look at the outside of a year's monthly parts lined up in sequence you will notice that each month seems to get fatter as the year goes on. This is not because there is more law made in, say, August or September than in January or February. It is on account of one of the principal virtues of *Current Law*: it is a *cumulative* reference work. Each monthly part gathers up all the law from the earlier parts and indexes it. It follows that you do not have to scour each monthly part in turn when researching for recent developments. You simply go straight to the end of the last monthly part and there find the index, which you will see covers the whole year up to then.

Browse a bit in one of the monthly parts to see its arrangement, and then find these other useful features:

(a) a name list of all the cases (shown in capitals) which have so far been reported this year, together with (in small type) all the existing cases which have been cited this year;

(b) a list of Acts continuing the *Legislation Citator* (see 13.6.2), i.e., every Act of whatever date to which something has happened this year;

(c) a list of all this year's SIs;

(d) a list of all the commencement dates which have been announced for Acts to come into force;

(e) a list of Parliamentary Bills and what stage in the legislative process they have reached;

(f) a list of all the year's assessments (by courts, not by agreement) of damages for personal injuries;

(g) a list of words and phrases which have received judicial attention this year.

Note that all these lists are also cumulative, so you should always consult just the latest and that will access the whole year's output.

13.3.2 *Current Law Yearbook*

At the end of the year these monthly parts are not bound up but discarded, when a *Current Law Yearbook* arrives (in about March), containing the twelve separate months' law reorganised into an annual volume, fully indexed and with additional matter. So if you know the approximate year of a particular happening in the law, by name or subject matter, CLYB can be a most effective quick reference source. It is additionally useful if you use the subject index because you will see that these tend to cumulate the last few years' CLYBs.

13.3.3 The *Current Law Citators*

We saw that the *Legislation Citator* and *Cases Citator*, each occupying three volumes, give the complete life history of all modern Acts and cases respectively, as well as the subsequent life history of any older Acts and cases which have had any 'life' in the years since 1947. It follows that when you have found your sought-after authority, it always pays to check its current status in the appropriate citator volume if it is more than a year old; and then in any event in the present year's *Current Law* running *Case Citator* or *Statute Citator*. You should then be up to date to the beginning of last month.

(While considering the *Current Law* service, we should also note that *Halsbury's Laws* offers some equivalent parts: monthly supplement booklets which are indexed cumulatively, and *Annual Abridgment* volumes similar in content to CLYB. These are a useful alternative source but on the whole *Current Law* is more comprehensive and easier to use.)

Still more recent developments, such as new SIs, progress of bills in Parliament, committee reports and very recent cases will be carried in the legal weeklies. Their case reports are fuller versions of reports which appeared a fortnight or so earlier in the broadsheet news-papers. The weeklies issue their own case indexes from time to time, but the better way of accessing these cases is through *Daily Law Reports Index*.

13.4 *DAILY LAW REPORTS INDEX*

This was mentioned earlier in connection with researching case law. We should note, however, that not only does it give us by name and by subject-matter every recent case of note, down to about last fortnight, but it also gives us every statute, SI, rule or regulation, EC directive or international convention, which has been the subject of reported litigation, accessed through its Legislation index.

13.5 *LEGAL JOURNALS INDEX*

Remembering that this indexes articles on every subject and that this includes case notes and statute notes, you will realise that this is a very useful research booster. If you are relying on a case or Act, old or recent, it is the work of only a few seconds to see if there has been something written about it recently. Your instinct should suggest to you when there will have been such recent commentary.

13.6 HOW DOES LAW GO OUT OF DATE?

This question may seem unnecessary or the answer obvious. However, a few moments considering it may help when it comes to constructive updating.

There are broadly four sorts of ways in which later legal change may affect earlier law. For simplicity we need consider only the interaction of statute and case law here; the effect of SIs will be considered further below.

13.6.1 Later case affecting earlier case

Apart from the obvious reversing (that is, in the same case at higher level) and overruling (that is, in a later case at higher level), this will be by the usual techniques of extending or distinguishing (that is, by varying the materiality of the earlier case's facts so as to widen or limit its application). The subsequent case history of every case can be found by searching in the *Current Law Case Citator* volume(s). This gives in a word ('followed', 'distinguished', 'doubted', etc.) the editors' assessment of the impact. Alternatively LEXIS CASES file will give every subsequent appearance of a case name but you will have to make your own assessment of the later courts' treatment of it.

13.6.2   Later statute affecting earlier statute

The endless process of amending, repealing and consolidating can be researched in *Current Law Legislation Citator* volume(s). Every statute of whatever date which has had any such attention since 1947 is listed, with its amendments and repeals of every section. (The officially-issued *Chronological Table* volumes also do this but are not usually so up to date.)

For the details of consolidations, you should refer to the tables of *derivations* (where did this vaguely familiar but new section come from?) and *destinations* (where has our old and much-loved section now gone to?) which draftsmen nowadays helpfully provide in the consolidating Acts themselves.

The advantage of using the *Current Law Legislation Citator* is that it also gives any SIs that have been issued to implement sections of statutes. It also covers the following areas.

13.6.3   Later case interpreting statute

These also are set out in the *Current Law Legislation Citator*, continued into the present year by the citator section of the *Current Law Statutes* loose-leaf binder, the comparable binder of *Halsbury's Statutes*, or by the pink index to the *Law Reports*. Of these *Current Law* tends to be the most up to date, but a double check can sometimes produce an interesting variant.

13.6.4   Later statute affecting case law

This is more difficult to detect, starting from scratch. If an Act has in effect overruled a line of cases, the appropriate textbook will set this out and explain it. However, it may have happened too recently, or the Act may have had a too peripheral or too speculative effect for it to be noted. One might have thought that at least where there was a specific statutory reversal of a case, *Current Law Case Citator* and *The Digest* would have told us this; but they do not. Since any such effect will probably have been pointed out and discussed in professional literature, perhaps before as well as after it happened, the indexes to the legal periodicals could help. But as mentioned earlier, we now have the ALLJNL file of LEXIS which covers the last few years of articles in LSG and NLJ, and in the *Estates Gazette* since 1991. This is probably the best place to detect this effect. If there is legislation bent on abolishing a common law rule, there is almost certain to be an article describing the legislation and, if there is, it is bound to mention the case or cases by name. A search for the case name should produce the article.

To take a simple current example: at the time of writing, a private member's Bill has just received the Royal Assent to become the Access to Neighbouring Land Act 1992. We have just received the Queen's Printer's copy but cannot expect an annotated version for quite some time. For any explanatory commentary on its merits and weaknesses, and which case or cases (on trespass?) it might have affected, we have at this moment only the journals for guidance. From the legislation index of LJI we are able to discover that it has had some commentary, for example, in the *Estates Gazette*. We can do this because we know the Bill by name, having seen it listed under 'legislation in progress' in the weeklies.

More typically, suppose we had not known of it. We have a problem involving the need to go on to neighbouring land to be able to do work on our own building, but the neighbours are uncooperative and have warned us not to trespass, referring us to the High Court case of *John Trenberth Ltd* v *National Westminster Bank* in 1979. When we check on this case we find it confirms that we have no means of getting access unless the neighbour consents, and that the Court of Appeal approved the decision in *Patel* v *W H Smith (Eziot) Ltd* [1987] 1 WLR 853.

It looks like we will have to advise our client either to offer to pay the neighbours whatever they ask for the privilege of access, or to somehow cope without such access. But it should occur to us to see what the profession thinks of these decisions. Not only might it suggest some ways round them but it might also reveal some later developments. Sure enough, by searching for *Trenberth* in the LEXIS ALLJNL file we accidentally find the new Bill mentioned and also Law Commission Report No. 151 (1985), because a commentator on the Bill quite naturally introduced it by express reference to the *Trenberth* ruling.

Fortunately, we rarely start from scratch in this sort of research. The likelihood is that legislation overhauling existing case law will be deliberate, and perhaps the result of public discussion, Parliamentary debate or committee report. While this is still recent, the chances are that you or a helpful colleague will recall the background, and once some time has elapsed the text writers should have covered it at least in their supplements.

Chapter Fourteen

European Community Legal Documents

The legal literature of the EC is vast and ever-increasing. A few official and university libraries have been designated European Documentation Centres and as such receive automatically all official publications of the various organs of the Community. The larger firms of solicitors and some chambers hold a selection of EC legal materials. The selection tends to be rather arbitrary and to vary greatly. See what your library has. You may find it has unofficial publications put out by commercial publishers: these can be more helpful than the EC's own sources. But find out where your nearest Documentation Centre is. (They are listed in the *Directory of EEC Information Sources* which law reference libraries should have.) See how it is organised and what the official legal documents look like.

Because of the multiplicity of books available and the wide variation of holdings possible, the sources and works listed in what follows is fuller than for other sections of this manual. Beginners should not be discouraged by this. Many of the commercial publications are overlapping and competing both among themselves and with the official publications. Consulting any one in each main field will probably be sufficient at the start, and anyway, you may only have one in your library. The task for beginners is to see what EC law consists of, how it is organised and how the tools available in their particular library may be used to find it.

If you did EC law in your degree course or other studies, you will know something about the structure and organs of the Community, and the lawmaking that results from these. If you do not know about these, you can best understand EC legal documents by making an analogy with UK law. The EC produces various types of law, corresponding broadly in type with our domestic law: primary legislation, secondary legislation, and case law. They are also comparable in the way they are either judicially noted or proved in our courts (see European Communities Act 1972, s. 3).

14.1   EC LEGISLATION

14.1.1   Primary legislation

This consists of the treaties which established the three communities (the Economic Community, the Coal and Steel Community (ECSC) and Euratom), various amending treaties, and the Single European Act. There is an official EC edition of these clad in the lilac livery which the EC has adopted for its official colour, called *Treaties Establishing the European Communities*. But in most libraries they may be found in *Halsbury's Statutes* Vol. 50 and *Supplement*, or in Sweet and Maxwell's *Encyclopaedia of European Community Law*, B volumes.

14.1.2   Secondary legislation

This consists of Regulations, Directives or Decisions. (For the difference between these, see Art. 189 of the EEC Treaty.) These are cited by their year, community and running number, e.g.,

Reg 123/88; Dir 85/123; Dec 89/123

Notice that regulations have their number first, the others their year first.

14.1.3   Finding secondary legislation

All EC secondary legislation, including draft legislation, and also recommendations and opinions, are published in the *Official Journal*

(OJ). This is the main organ and official gazette of the EC. In theory, with a reference to a particular instrument, it can be found in the OJ via its index (in alphabetical order, by subject) or methodological table (in numerical order, for each type of instrument). In practice this may be difficult. One reason is that, with the OJ now running to about 32 volumes a year, few libraries can shelve the entire set or more than a few recent years' volumes. (However, libraries can now get it on microfiche, and so need to take just the current year in paper parts.) Another reason is that the indexing is slow and is only by the month and by the single year, not cumulated.

14.1.4 The L and C Series

There are now separate series within the OJ. The L series contains legislation and is therefore the part you are most likely to want. The C series contains a mixed bag of non-legislative matter including the decisions (not the judgments – just their outcome) of the European Court, official announcements, opinions of the Parliament on preparatory drafts from the Council of Ministers or the Commission (but not actual Parliamentary debates, which appear in another Annex series). However, it is in the C series that draft legislation is published, so you may have to grapple with it.

14.1.5 Secondary legislation from commercial publishers

Various commercial publishers have stepped in to fill the gap in the market with a more accessible collection of texts, including EC secondary legislation. In this country there are Sweet and Maxwell's loose-leaf multi-volume *Encyclopaedia of European Community Law* C volumes, and the American-inspired CCH *Common Market Reporter*, also loose-leaf.

14.1.6 Is it in force?

EC secondary legislation is constantly amended and supplemented. As with UK legislation you must check to see the present state of any particular instrument. The EC publishes a *Directory of Community Legislation in Force* twice a year. Vol. 1 contains an Analytical Register, classifying by subject-matter. Vol. 2 has a chronological index, for when you know the reference number, and a broad subject category alphabetical index, which is useful for getting into the subject-matter headings used by Vol. 1.

Again, a more up to date and easier-to-use service is provided by commercial publishers: Butterworths offer *European Communities Legislation: Current Status* in 3 volumes, supplemented by fortnightly blue sheets and a telephone service for subscribers and North-Holland (Amsterdam) have their *Guide to EEC Legislation* which they supplement by a telex service.

14.1.7 1992 and all that

Much of our current quest for EC law is specifically for the legislation which promotes the single market. The EC in collaboration with UK publishers Graham and Trotman has provided its own official compilation in six massive loose-leaf volumes: *Completing the Internal Market of the European Community*. This consists of selected pages from the OJ, classified under subject headings. Also loose-leaf but more descriptive is the two-volume *Croner's Europe*, dealing with the business as well as the legal aspects of the single market.

There are any number of one-off monographs by UK bodies and individuals on the impact of the 1992 legislation. It would be pointless to list them here. See which your library has chosen.

14.1.8 Subject-headings

Searching for EC legislation by subject-matter can be difficult because the legal vocabulary of the Community is more varied and at times more obscure than our own. Some help can be got from the *Eurovoc* volumes which come as a companion to the OJ. These are a thesaurus: alphabetical, subject oriented and multi-lingual, to aid in word and concept searching. However, the soft-cover index volume of the *Current Status* set is probably a better place to start searching for EC secondary legislation by subject-matter.

14.1.9 General indexes

Halsbury's Laws new Vol. 53 has a set of tables for every sort of non-case material in the whole set. It separates the EC content into:

EC treaties; decisions and directives; regulations; and 'other material' (mainly notices and resolutions, and rules of procedure of ECJ). These lists are far from exhaustive but do include every mention of these documents occurring in the set, so should alert you to all such materials having any noticeable impact on UK law.

14.1.10   Implementation of Directives

Directives from Brussels tell member governments to legislate but leave them to do it in their national way. It may be easy enough to find the directive but often difficult to find if it has been put into law by the UK, let alone by other member states; and if so, how. Butterworths have recently brought out their *EC Legislation Implementor*, a soft-cover twice-yearly volume which sets out most of the EC's directives between the UK's accession and December 1991 (continued by the fortnightly blue sheets: see 14.1.6) giving for each the instrument of implementation by the UK. The book does not give directives which are unimplemented, or apparently unimplemented. This could mean they are not done yet; or do not need to be done because our law already covered them in substance; or were done by some laconic SI which did not say so; or were taken care of by some internal administrative instruction, for example, by the Bank of England.

There is also a table showing implementations (including non- and mis-implementations) by all twelve member states. This is taken from information published from time to time in the OJ, so while it is very useful as a positive check, its negative information may not be up to date.

If your library does not have this new book, you can detect implementation by one of the on-line services (see 14.6). Otherwise you may have to fall back on the *Halsbury's Laws* Vol. 53 indexes.

14.1.11   Draft legislation

We often need to know about proposals for new directives which are making their way through the EC's various organs. These are not always easy to find. Generally speaking, the Commission proposes and the Council eventually disposes, but the progress can be tortuous. The Commission's proposals first appear in their numbered COM series. These should be noted in the various current news sources (see 14.4.1), and are carried by the *House of Commons Weekly Information Bulletin*, which some law firms take especially for these EC pages. The proposals may go to the European Parliament and also to the Economic and Social Committee, in which case their discussion of them will appear in due course in the OJ's C Series. As noted earlier, however, the OJ index requires you to know the month or year. The Commission may then have second thoughts and put out its amended proposals in a further COM document. At the time of writing, the Commission's amended directive on unfair terms in consumer contracts has appeared as COM (92) 66, accepting some opinions and rejecting others. When finally adopted, the directive will appear in the OJ's L Series.

14.2 EC CASE LAW

Decisions of the European Court at Luxembourg (abbreviated CJEC or ECJ) and the more recently formed Court of First Instance (CFI) are reported in an official series, the *European Court Reports* (ECR). However, these are very slow to appear and are not well indexed. A few libraries get transcripts of judgments straight from Luxembourg. These are the quickest of all their reports – but you may have to translate them from French! A compromise, slightly less up to date, is the Court's *Proceedings* series, which come weekly in duplicated sheets, about three months after the decisions. These summarise case facts and extract the substance of the judgments.

More useful for most purposes are the *Common Market Law Reports* (CMLR), and they also include relevant decisions of the courts of member states. Some libraries have the CCH *Common Market Reporter*, mentioned earlier. This gives selected recent cases in its loose-leaf parts and these are then collected and published in a bound companion series, *European Community Cases* cited as CEC.

14.2.1 Digests of case law

14.2.1.1 *Digest of Case Law*

The EC is in the process of producing a loose-leaf *Digest of Case Law* which seeks to summarise the effect of decisions: of the CJEC in an

A series; of member states' courts in a B series; of cases concerning EC officials in a C series; and of cases involving the Brussels Convention (on conflicts of jurisdiction and judgments between member states) in a D series. The digests extract and quote the essential statements of law.

14.2.1.2   *The Gazetteer of European Law: Case Search series*

This is produced in two volumes continued monthly and attempts to provide up to date summaries. It indexes cumulatively throughout the year.

14.2.1.3   *The Digest*

We saw earlier (11.1) that this has a European volume, Vol. 21. It cannot be as comprehensive as the specialised sources but may have enough of a particular case you have been referred to to spare you a trip to a more specialised library. Even with its supplement, however, do not take it as the last word.

14.2.2   Finding EC cases

As with other EC documents, decisions of the Court of Justice or Court of First Instance of the EC are officially listed by number within their year, starting with case 1/54. However, we tend to refer to EC cases in various ways, and rarely by these numbers: they have of course their parties' names (mostly unmemorable and often unpronounceable); they often have nicknames (the Volvo case, the potato starch case, etc.); or we may recall them only by their subject-matter. And then again we may want to know if there has been a case on a particular Treaty article, Directive, Regulation, or whatever. For accessing EC cases from any of these starting-points the *Gazetteer* (14.2.1.2) and its monthly parts index under these separate heads, and cumulatively throughout each year. Alternatively, there is now an excellent new one-volume guide: Butterworths' *EC Case Citator 1991-92*. It is based on the ECR and CMLR, but also gives OJ references to assist in finding cases not in those series. Butterworths continue it with a fortnightly *Case Citator Service*, pink sheets listing all the most recent cases by number, name and subject area. The *Citator* is easier to use than the *Gazetteer* but it only gives citations, not digests. The *Gazetteer* however, also attempts to follow up earlier cases where they are referred to in later ones.

14.3   PERIODICAL LITERATURE

A large number of official periodicals emanate from various organs of the EC. The most important general one is the monthly *Bulletin of the European Communities*. Various publishers produce their own journals: *Common Market Law Review, European Law Review, Journal of Common Market Studies*, etc. All significant articles on EC law relevant to the UK are indexed in *Current Law* (9.1) and *Legal Journals Index* (9.2).

14.4   GENERAL SURVEYS OF EC LAW

There are now many textbooks by individual authors explaining EC law and legal structure to beginners, as well as monographs on particular aspects, e.g., competition. Every library differs in its holdings of these, but all will have *Halsbury's Laws* Vols 51 and 52 and *Supplement*, which attempt to give a wide-ranging survey of all aspects of EC law, as part of their encyclopaedic treatment of English law. The same content appears as a separate loose-leaf work, Vaughan's *Law of the European Communities Service*. Similar in general scope is another loose-leaf cumulating text in four volumes: *EEC Brief* edited by Myles and published in Northern Ireland. *Croner's Europe*, yet another loose-leaf text in two volumes, concentrates more on the legal and business aspects of the single market.

14.5   REGULAR NEWS BULLETINS

Such is the ferment of EC lawmaking, proposals and commentaries that several publishers offer monthly, weekly, or even daily newssheets of current legal intelligence. The following are just a few examples.

14.5.1   *EC Brief*

Butterworths began publishing in 1989 their *EC Brief*, a weekly newsletter reporting legal happenings of every sort, supported by a telephone service. This is recast into an annual volume summarising all EC (and related UK) legal happenings, proposals, publications, etc., over the year: the equivalent of a *Current Law Year Book* or a *Halsbury's Annual Abridgment*, confined to EC developments.

14.5.2   *Common Market Reporter*

CCH, whose multi-volume *Common Market Reporter* was mentioned before (14.1.5 and 14.2), also publishes a fortnightly information booklet of the same name.

14.5.3   *Europe*

A pink news-sheet simply called *Europe* comes almost daily from the publishers Agence Europe. It covers a wide range of world news affecting Europe as well as EC developments and has a vigorous editorial style. Its text is also available on-line so that it should in theory be possible to find any particular piece of information without having to wade through a large batch of sheets.

14.5.4   *European Access*

This is published six times a year by Chadwyck-Healey and gives very detailed references and some useful descriptions of current EC activities, literature and comment.

14.5.5   *Current Law* and *European Current Law*

Current Law for some years has had a 'European Communities' subject heading which covers the month's legal developments. These then appear in *Current Law Year Book*. (There are similar sections in the monthly digest parts of *Halsbury's Laws* and its *Annual Abridgment*.) However, from 1992 there is now a specialised version, *European Current Law* covering every country in Europe (save Turkey), cumulating monthly and with a yearbook. If it fulfils its promises, this could become the most useful source to hand in almost all law libraries for updating on all aspects of the law of the entire continent. If your library does not take it, it would be well to remember that the ordinary *Current Law* will now contain rather less European matter than formerly. Conversely, *Current Law* will continue to list major articles on European law, because the new publication does not list any periodical articles at all.

14.6 COMPUTER DATABASES

There is now a bewildering array of on-line databases which have EC materials. You may come across any of Celex, Spearhead, Scad, Info 92, Sesame, Eurocron, Cedefop, Echo, Cordis, Polis, Eclas and many others; and Eurobases, Profile, Nexis, Justis, and other means of plugging into them. Which of these your library may have, what these offer and how to use them must be for the librarians to explain, and even then is probably best left for them to use on your behalf. However, since you are likely to be using LEXIS, you should note how it also accesses EC materials.

14.6.1 LEXIS

LEXIS has its European Communities library, EURCOM. This has CASES and COMDEC files. CASES has all the ECR and CMLR reports since these series began as well as other series such as *European Commercial Cases* and *European Human Rights Reports*. COMDEC has all the decisions of the Commission on competition matters, mainly under Articles 85 and 86. In addition LEXIS now has an INTLAW library which includes an ECLAW file containing much of the OJ L and C Series. Details of these libraries are in the literature supplied to subscribers by LEXIS. (See further Chapter 16.)

14.6.2 Celex

The EC has its own official database, Celex. This is organised into eight sectors, covering virtually the whole of the EC's massive legislative, judicial and preparatory output, and almost all in full text. Documentation Centres and some large firms have it direct. Other libraries get into it, or parts of it, through LEXIS or Profile. Parts of Celex are now also offered on CD-ROM (video disc), with regular updates. Celex should in time become not only the most up to date and complete source of EC legal information, but also the most universally accessible.

14.6.3 Spearhead

Spearhead is another much-favoured database. It summarises legislation related to the single market, at every stage of its life cycle from the merely projected to the fully implemented. One of its special virtues is that because it is produced by the DTI, it gives the names of responsible officials to contact at government level.

14.7 DIAGRAM

A diagram indicating a suggested sequence for researching into EC law is provided in Chapter 17.

EXERCISE M: EUROPEAN COMMUNITY LAW

1. Find out what the following are about and whether they are still in force:

1686/75/EEC, 87/153/EEC, 3104/87/EEC

2. What is 3626/82 about? Has there been any case law interpreting it?

3. Find a report of the *Gingerbread* case.

4. Which is the EC Directive which gave rise to the Consumer Protection Act 1987? Who signed it?

5. Has the EC had anything to say about dangerous substances in batteries? If so, how if at all is UK law affected?

6. The CJEC four or five years ago ruled that the Commission, having mistakenly awarded too large an amount of aid to an applicant, could not after two years withdraw the award and make a fresh one for a lesser amount. What was the case? Who was the Advocate-General in the case?

7. Your client has a small commercial airline which flies freight to and from Europe and North America in jet-powered aircraft. Some

of his planes are quite old. He understands there is some EC law
about the maximum noise they are allowed to make. He would like
to be advised if it applies to his operations.

Chapter Fifteen

International and Foreign Law

Sooner or later your legal researches may take you far from home and into foreign parts.

15.1 EUROPEAN COMMUNITY LAW

We have looked briefly at the sources of EC law, but its treaties, directives, regulations and case law must anyway be regarded for all purposes as UK law: see European Communities Act 1972, s. 3.

15.2 FOREIGN LAW

15.2.1 Application of foreign law

The law of a foreign country (including, for some purposes, that of Scotland, Ireland, the Channel Isles and Isle of Man) can crop up in many ways, e.g., in an international commercial agreement, foreign will, conveyance or divorce, tortious act occurring abroad, dealings with property situated overseas etc. If any such have to be construed or litigated, reference to the relevant foreign legal rules may be necessary. The body of English law which applies to rights or wrongs involving a foreign element is called Conflict of Laws, or Private International Law. This has developed common law rules as to how such problems are to be resolved and the manner in which our law or the appropriate foreign law is to be applied. There are now various statutes and international conventions also applicable.

The standard practitioners' work in this field is *Dicey and Morris*. There are also various academic works and monographs on specific aspects of the subject. For litigation within one or more EC member states, their courts' organisation, procedure, enforcement, etc., useful guides are O'Malley and Layton's *European Civil Practice* and Vaughan's *Guide to European Court Practice*.

15.2.2   Ascertainment of foreign law

Where foreign law has to be researched, an expert may be needed. There are directories of such experts in most practitioners' libraries and some firms maintain their own in-house lists. If there is to be litigation, the effect of the foreign law must either be agreed or proved by evidence from the expert. (Foreign law is treated as fact, not law, by our courts, and is therefore the subject of expert evidence. See Civil Evidence Act 1972, s. 4(1) on qualifications of foreign law experts, and 4(2) on reliance on previous findings of foreign law.)

However, before approaching an expert it may be wise to obtain an outline of the foreign law applicable. The LEXIS database holds law from Scotland, Ireland, France, Commonwealth countries, and of course the USA. But it is not always straightforward to use if you are not certain exactly what you are seeking. There are of course many one-country or one-region monographs now available which set out the trading or other law of, e.g., Japan or the Gulf. However, a general source for first acquaintance is in *Martindale-Hubbell*. This is a directory in many huge volumes of the US legal profession. Larger law firms here have it in their libraries. After it has finally finished listing all the US lawyers it has further volumes containing useful summaries of the distinctive law of each State in USA, and then of most other countries. Look for the volume which says *Canadian and International Law Digest* on the spine and you will see the coverage.

Do not forget that *European Current Law* (14.5.5) covers the whole of the continent, not just the EC. It means that for the first time in ordinary English law libraries there is a constant and easily- accessed cumulating survey of foreign law of a significant portion of the world.

15.3 INTERNATIONAL LAW

This is concerned with the rules governing the relations between states, areas of the world such as sea and air lying outside domestic law, the laws of war and peace, and so forth. Some of its sources are in judicial decisions or international custom and practice; but the source you are most likely to be looking for will be some international convention or treaty. Those treaties most frequently referred to should be found in the appropriate textbooks on, e.g., aviation or maritime law. Some are actually appended to the Act of Parliament which formally incorporated them into UK law. A useful index is in Vol. 53 of *Halsbury's Laws* where all treaties and conventions mentioned anywhere in the set will be listed in the appropriate table.

15.3.1 Indexes of treaties

The best key to all treaties and conventions of general importance – over 1000 of them – is Bowman and Harris's *Multilateral Treaties* (1984 with 1990 *Supplement*). This lists them both in date order and by subject-matter, and indicates where their text is published. HMSO in 1970 published in three volumes Parry and Hopkins's *Index of British Treaties 1101-1968*. This lists all treaties affecting this country down to that year, chronologically, by subject and by country.

15.3.2 Maritime conventions

For the very many maritime conventions, shipping lawyers' libraries have either Singh's *International Maritime Law Conventions* or the American *Benedict on Admiralty*.

15.3.3 In-house files

Remember that unless it is a very new convention you are after, the chances are that it has already been sought repeatedly by others before you. So always inquire to see if it has been copied into your firm's or chambers' own compiled in-house materials.

15.3.4   LEXIS INTLAW Library

This offers a very useful range of both international and foreign legal materials. In particular, its BDIEL file (basic documents of international economic law) includes the texts of many of the most important multilateral treaties and conventions. See the LEXIS literature for full contents of this and other files on INTLAW.

EXERCISE N: FOREIGN AND INTERNATIONAL LAW

1.   Is the International Cocoa Agreement 1980 binding on the UK?

2.   Your client, a sports goods manufacturer who exports to various countries, is proposing to launch a new line of sports equipment using as a logo the olympic symbol. Advise him if he is safe to go ahead.

3.   Under Swedish law, which documents are required to be under seal?

4.   The *MV Shortfuse* sailed for a port in the Middle East with a cargo of chemical fertiliser. During the voyage the crew accidentally discovered explosives and detonators in some of the containers. On the Master's orders, these containers were thrown overboard. The cargo owners are now suing saying that he had no right to do this, and that he acted in an unnecessarily drastic and hasty manner. Was the Master entitled in maritime law to act as he did?

5.   Klang GMBH, a German company with an office in London, entered into an agreement with Bell & Lever, the London subsidiary of a US corporation, for the supply of components for double-glazing units. The contract was expressed to be governed by English law. Bell & Lever say that the parts supplied have been defective and have caused them considerable loss in extra work and cancelled orders. They want to sue Klang in England. Klang, who deny liability, say that under the Brussels Convention they can only be sued in Germany. They point out that they also have a counterclaim against Bell & Lever, which is certainly not justiciable in England. Advise Bell & Lever whether they should start proceedings here or in Germany.

6. Grieff SA, a company incorporated under French law, agreed with Rink Inc, a US corporation, to act as distributors in various European countries, including UK, of skating equipment made and supplied by Rink. The UK part of the contract was expressed to be governed by English law. Grieff wish to sue Rink in England for failure to perform their part of the contract. Can they go ahead? If the Rome Convention (1980) is applicable, would this make any difference?

7. What limit does Poland's Commercial Code Amendment Act 1991 place on the share capital of a limited liability company?

Chapter Sixteen

On-Line Researching

No lawyers today can count themselves well-equipped researchers unless they have some facility with the various computerised and other electronic sources now on tap. Yet apart from LEXIS, these seem still to be mostly the preserve of law librarians. Perhaps this is as it should be: one needs to be using these things every day to get skilled in using them, and few lawyers are so frequently involved with them in the way their librarians are. Nevertheless we need to know of their existence and scope, and how to access them. (We also need to be aware of their cost!)

16.1 LEXIS

This is not an attempt to teach you how to use LEXIS. You have to attend a training session or two, study thoroughly the guides and literature supplied by LEXIS and gain experience using a terminal. The notes and examples which follow assume that you have had that initial introduction and offer some guidance as to when LEXIS is likely to help, either initially or after a hard-copy start.

16.2 LEXIS GUIDES

If you have attended a course but now feel you have forgotten what you learned – a common experience – a good brief reminder is in

Dane & Thomas' *How to Use a Law Library*. LEXIS issue an outline guide with periodic updates; you are entitled to a copy if you have a LEXIS number. The fullest guides to the contents of LEXIS are published in the USA, but there the database is wider than that offered by the British licensees, Butterworths. Likewise the fullest and most readable guide to the use of LEXIS, Shapiro's *LEXIS, the Complete User's Guide* (New York 1989), is well worth getting for just its first 150 pages of search technique, after which most of the book is about American sources.

16.3 WHAT LEXIS CONTAINS

16.3.1 The English General Library

This library, accessed as ENGGEN, will probably be your most frequent LEXIS resource with its CASES and STATIS files. Make yourself familiar with its scope and limitations. Note especially what it has that ordinary libraries have not (e.g. the Court of Appeal (Civil) transcripts of unreported cases since 1980), and *vice-versa* what it lacks, (e.g. older reports, and pre-1980 cases reported only in the *Criminal Law Review*).

16.3.2 The UKJNL Library

This most important addition to the database gives access to the contents of the *New Law Journal* and *Law Society's Gazette* since 1986, and the *Estates Gazette* from 1991. Among that material are numerous articles describing changes in the law, actual, foreseen or speculative. One especial updating advantage of this was mentioned earlier: anything significant affecting existing cases or statutes will almost certainly have been spotted and commented on by somebody. Say, for example, the rule in *Hedley Byrne* v *Heller* was cut down or extended in a particular direction by a new case. You could of course find this by conventional searching. But if a statute, law reform report, government white paper, EC Directive, or whatever has any impact, actual or anticipated, on the principle laid down in *Hedley Byrne*, a likely way of detecting this would be by calling up UKJNL library, selecting the ALLJNL file, putting in the case name and seeing if it has had any flicker of life in the recent past. To repeat the

example given in 13.6.4, giving the 1979 case as *Trenberth* to the
ALLJNL file will reveal an article in 1991 on the Access to
Neighbouring Land Bill and also the Law Commission Report
which surveyed the law some years ago.

16.3.3 Ever-wider horizons

LEXIS started in the USA and its centre of gravity remains in US
law, but it has a great deal of material from the rest of the common
law world and from France and other countries. It is now expanding
its EC and international database with its INTLAW library. The
INTLAW files include ECLAW which accesses the Celex database,
including the OJ of the EC going back many years, important
collections of International Law documents, conventions, treaties,
etc. in the BDIEL and ILMTY files, and even Chinese law in the
CHINAL file. The case law of the EC has been available to UK
LEXIS users for some time via the EURCOM library. It can now
also be accessed through INTLAW.

16.3.4 How up to date?

The time-lag for LEXIS updating can be several weeks. For the most
recent happenings in for example, statutes and SIs, LAWTEL (see
16.5.2) is usually quicker. *Daily Law Reports Index* is more up to date
than LEXIS for cases.

16.4 USING LEXIS: THINGS TO REMEMBER

16.4.1 How LEXIS thinks

Remember that LEXIS contains no law. It only contains words. To
make it work effectively for you, think of it as a vast collection of
words. All LEXIS can do is to compare the words or combinations
you choose to give it with those it has, offering you any that
correspond. It is therefore totally literal and you have to think the
same way.

For example, I wanted to find what cases there had been in the last
twelve months in which the 'state of the art' defence in product

liability had been raised, to see the courts' present attitude. This is just the sort of word-search at which LEXIS is so much better and quicker than any conventional method. I asked for 'state w/5 art and date aft June 1991'. This produced several useful cases. As one was in the House of Lords, I called it up. It was *Union Transport Group* v *Continental Lines* [1992] 1 WLR 15; 1 All ER 161. The phrase I was seeking occurs as '. . . the appellants, being domiciled in Belgium, which is of course a contracting state, invoked art. 2 of the convention . . .'. You can see from this how simply literal LEXIS is.

16.4.2 How lawyers use words

The words of the law can come in two distinct styles: judges' and legislators'. These may be quite different from each other, even on the same subject-matter, e.g. a judge will call non-hearsay evidence 'original', whereas the Civil Evidence Act 1968 and Criminal Justice Act 1988 call it 'direct'. Conversely judges and draftsmen may use the same word with different meanings, as when 'assault' in all the criminal statutes virtually means battery, but in the courts' parlance means only asssault: *DPP* v *Taylor* [1992] 2 WLR 460; 1 All ER 299. Keep this possibility in mind when trying out words on the CASES and STATIS files respectively.

16.4.3 What LEXIS does best

16.4.3.1 *Finding the presence of words*

LEXIS works best, easily beating hard-copy research, where the use of an unusual and significant word or phrase, whether legal usage or otherwise, is being sought. Where on the other hand a problem concerns everyday legal concepts and vocabulary, it will need two or three levels of refinement; and even then you may still have to scroll through many cases before finding one relevant. In the latter instance, hard-copy research may well prove quicker than LEXIS, because the practised human eye is far from superseded as a rapid scanner of columns and footnotes. The two exercise problems at the end of this section exemplify this point.

16.4.3.2 *Finding the definition of words*

LEXIS can be very useful for finding instances where a word or phrase has received statutory or judicial construction. But unless it is a highly unusual and rarely-occurring term you would do well to remember the advice in 6.8 about the need to connect it to the various synonyms for 'meaning'.

16.4.4 The need to plan ahead

You should always have what LEXIS calls a search strategy worked out in advance. Consider which keywords with which connectors would seem most pomising, and then try to devise and have in reserve a second-level to refine your search should this be necessary. Before approaching the terminal, consider whether you can do some preliminary ground-clearing in the library which will help you to pose the right questions (and to understand LEXIS's answers – or failure to answer!). For example, almost any of the earlier exercises in this book can be done for useful practice on LEXIS. There may however, be the same initial difficulty as noted in the problems in Exercise H (page 63) where no keyword is apparent. In H 1. LEXIS will offer nothing relevant in exchange for 'drinks' or 'drinks AND machine'. 'Landlord OR tenan! w/20 meal!' might have been better. But a reference to the books first, for an overview of the law, would have revealed 'board'. This is of course a word used in many contexts in the law. So you would still need some forethought to devise an apt association and connector to get to the case in point.

EXERCISE O: RESEARCHING WITH LEXIS

There is some relevant case law on the following problems. Try finding it by LEXIS. But first think how you would find it by conventional searching.

1. Your opinion is sought by Green, who has a garden centre situated in an outer London suburb. He intends to fly a captive helium balloon above the garden centre as an advertisement. He would like to fly it as high as possible. He wants it there for the whole

summer season. He intends to tie it to the roof of a caravan which he has on the site. Can he go ahead?

2. Your opinion is sought by Brown. He is a tenant under a lease which has a covenant 'not to assign or underlet any part of the premises without the written consent of the landlord'. Brown intends to sublet the entire premises to one sublessee. Brown says that he does not need any consent for this, since he is not underletting a 'part' but the whole. Is he right?

16.5 OTHER DATABASES

Among the many others, you are most likely to come across JUSTIS and LAWTEL. Some law firms also have databases which are not specifically for law, such as Profile and Textline.

16.5.1 JUSTIS

We mentioned various other databases like Celex and Spearhead when we were looking at EC legal documents (14.6.2 and 14.6.3). They can both be accessed through JUSTIS, and this also has CMLR, WLR, the LR red index, Criminal Appeal Office indexes, and daily reports from *The Times* and *Independent*.

16.5.2 LAWTEL

Looks like an ordinary TV teletext, which is what it is, receiving a specialised sub-service of BT's Prestel service. It has English cases and statutes from 1980, Bills currently in Parliament, SIs from 1983, and much other useful legal intelligence, which is updated daily.

16.5.3 Profile

This is produced by the *Financial Times*. It contains a wide range of UK and overseas newspapers and magazines offering economic, financial, industrial, scientific and general business and current affairs news. It also includes Spearhead and the part of Celex which contains the 1992 legislation affecting the UK.

16.5.4 Textline

This is produced by Reuters. Its main purpose is to provide information for business. To do this it covers more than 2,000 newspapers, magazines and journals from around the world starting from 1980. This makes it very useful indeed for secondary legal research.

Chapter Seventeen

Diagrams

Some people find a sequence of operations easier to follow and to remember if it is presented visually as well as verbally. Others find diagrams and flow charts add little to or even lessen their understanding. The following three diagrams are therefore entirely optional. In the nature of such things they are over-simplified and merely repeat what has appeared in the text, which of course remains essential for understanding. Nevertheless I hope they may be found helpful by some readers – who should very soon be able to dispense with them anyway.

17.1   BASIC PROBLEM-SOLVING

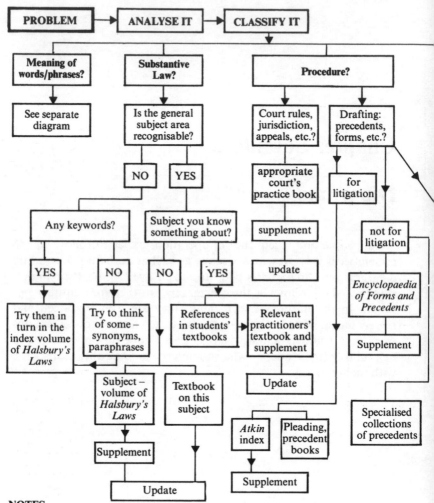

NOTES

1. This diagram is only a rudimentary outline, indicating some of the main directions that might usefully be pursued in legal problem solving. In so far as you find that it states the obvious, you must already have some skill or instinct for basic legal research.

2. Where, having followed one particular line, the result suggests that your original classification was incorrect, go back and recommence at the appropriate heading.

3. 'Supplement' means that you must refer efficiently to all the supplement(s) and services supplied with the source indicated.

4. 'Update' means go through the appropriate updating procedures, some of which are indicated under the 'Law Known' heading.

5. LEXIS-searching may be useful at many points, either initially or once a certain amount of information has been obtained. LEXIS has been left out of the diagram, however, to avoid overloading it.

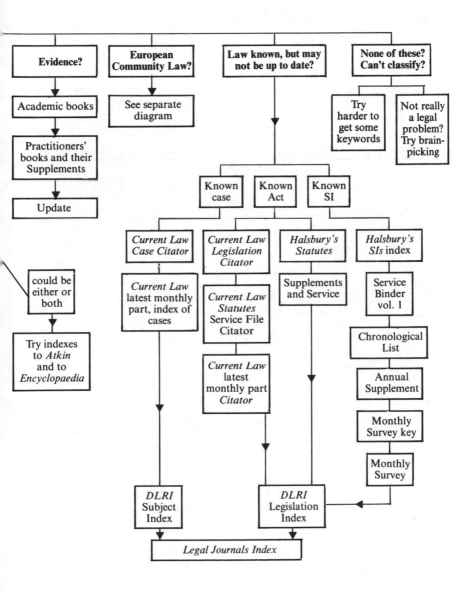

Evidence?

European Community Law?

Law known, but may not be up to date?

None of these? Can't classify?

Academic books

See separate diagram

Try harder to get some keywords

Not really a legal problem? Try brain-picking

Practitioners' books and their Supplements

Update

Known case

Known Act

Known SI

Current Law Case Citator

Current Law Legislation Citator

Halsbury's Statutes

Halsbury's SIs index

could be either or both

Current Law latest monthly part, index of cases

Current Law Statutes Service File Citator

Supplements and Service

Service Binder vol. 1

Try indexes to Atkin and to Encyclopaedia

Current Law latest monthly part Citator

Chronological List

Annual Supplement

Monthly Survey key

Monthly Survey

DLRI Subject Index

DLRI Legislation Index

Legal Journals Index

17.2 RESEARCHING EUROPEAN COMMUNITY LAW

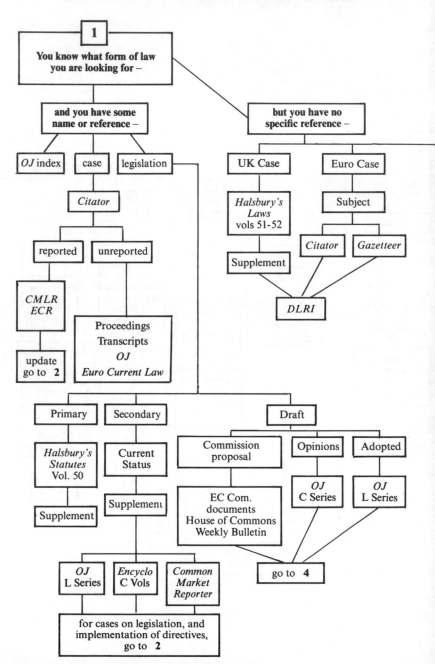

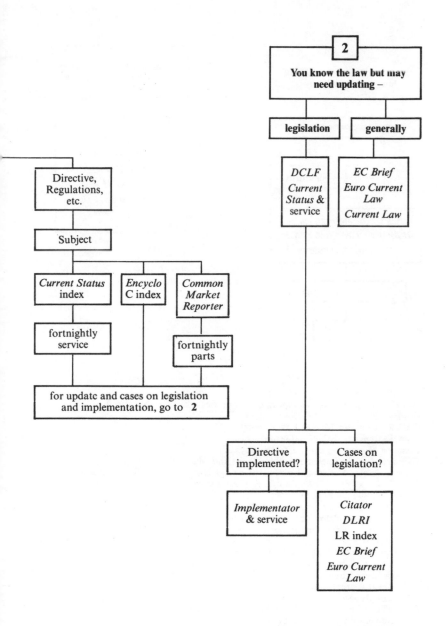

(Diagram continued over.)

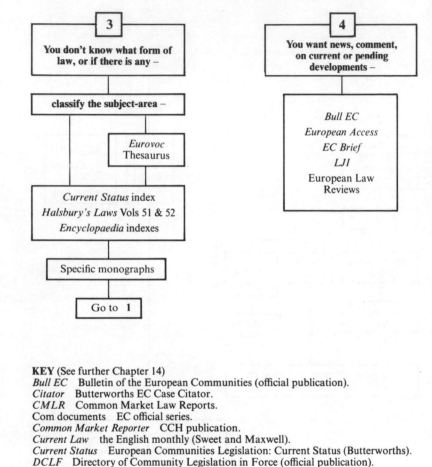

KEY (See further Chapter 14)
Bull EC   Bulletin of the European Communities (official publication).
Citator   Butterworths EC Case Citator.
CMLR   Common Market Law Reports.
Com documents   EC official series.
Common Market Reporter   CCH publication.
Current Law   the English monthly (Sweet and Maxwell).
Current Status   European Communities Legislation: Current Status (Butterworths).
DCLF   Directory of Community Legislation in Force (official publication).
DLRI   Daily Law Reports Index.
EC Brief   European Community Brief (Butterworths).
ECR   European Court Reports (official publication).
Encyclopaedia   Encyclopaedia of European Community Law (Sweet and Maxwell).
Euro Current-Law   European Current Law (Sweet and Maxwell).
European Access   Chadwyck-Healey publication.
Gazetteer   Gazetteer of European Law – Case Search Series (European Law Centre).
Implementator   Butterworths EC Legislation Implementator.
LJI   Legal Journals Index.
LR   Law Reports
OJ   Official Journal of the European Communities.
Proceedings   European Court (Official Publication).
Transcripts   European Court (Official Publication).

17.3 WORDS AND PHRASES IN STATUTES, ETC.

There follows a suggested sequence for construing their meaning. It may also be used for construing documents, by analogy; and when drafting you own. The sequence may not need to be followed through every stage if a definition or interpretation is revealed early, e.g., in the annotations to a statute. Similarly, if a meaning before or after a specific date is sought, *CLYB* or *Halsbury's* Annual Abridgment may be a useful approach.

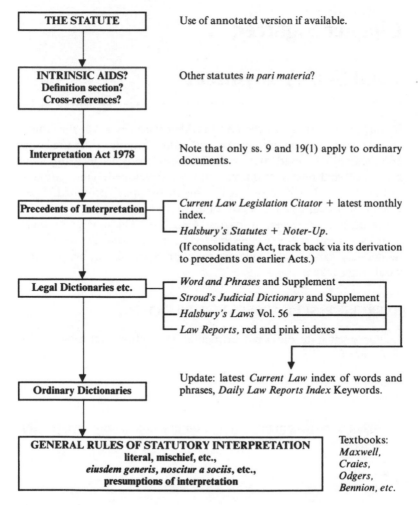

THE STATUTE	Use of annotated version if available.
INTRINSIC AIDS? Definition section? Cross-references?	Other statutes *in pari materia*?
Interpretation Act 1978	Note that only ss. 9 and 19(1) apply to ordinary documents.
Precedents of Interpretation	*Current Law Legislation Citator* + latest monthly index. *Halsbury's Statutes* + *Noter-Up*. (If consolidating Act, track back via its derivation to precedents on earlier Acts.)
Legal Dictionaries etc.	*Word and Phrases* and Supplement *Stroud's Judicial Dictionary* and Supplement *Halsbury's Laws* Vol. 56 *Law Reports*, red and pink indexes
Ordinary Dictionaries	Update: latest *Current Law* index of words and phrases, *Daily Law Reports Index* Keywords.
GENERAL RULES OF STATUTORY INTERPRETATION literal, mischief, etc., *eiusdem generis, noscitur a sociis*, etc., presumptions of interpretation	Textbooks: *Maxwell, Craies, Odgers, Bennion, etc.*

Chapter Eighteen

Final Self-Assessment

If you have read and absorbed and tackled the exercises to this point, you should be getting quite proficient at law finding. Here are some exercises with focused and unfocused problems to measure how much skill and resourcefulness you have developed. Time yourself against the clock and record your time in the space provided. Then when you have done all of them, or all that you have been able to do, check the answers, given on pages 143 to 146. The time given there with each answer is a suggested 'par for the course': the time a moderately experienced lawyer, familiar with his or her library, would have taken.

EXERCISE P: SELF-ASSESSMENT TEXT

1. On what date did Environmental Protection Act 1990, s. 99 come into force?

answer:
time taken:

2. What is the maximum sentence on first conviction for tattooing a minor?

answer:
time taken:

3. Which 1990 case decided that a wine seller could avoid conviction for false trade description where the wine producer had incorrectly labelled the bottle?

answer
time taken:

4. What is SI 1991/961 about?

answer:
time taken

5. What is RSC Order 84 about?

answer:
time taken:

6. What exactly does a right of pannage allow to be eaten?

answer:
time taken:

7. Find the form required for applying to open a zoo. To whom does one apply? How long would the licence last if granted?

answer:
time taken:

8. Who were the solicitors in *Walsh* v *Lonsdale*?

answer:
time taken:

9. Find the most recent reported case on insider dealing.

answer:
time taken:

10. Advise whether an aumbry is legal.

   answer:
   time taken

11. Client contracted to buy a house. After contracts were ex-
changed the house suffered flood damage. There is now some dispute
with the vendor as to who should bear the cost of repairs. You seem
to recall a useful summary of the present law was contained in a fairly
recent Law Commission report. See if you can find the report by a
methodical search.

   answer:
   time taken:

12. A solicitor supplied a reference for a client at the request of a
third party who was seeking to do business with the client. The
solicitor's reference did not mention matters which would have
affected the third party's willingness to trust the client. This was
because the solicitor felt he would be betraying his client's confid-
ences. The third party, having lost money in reliance on the
reference, now wants to sue the solicitor for negligence. Can you find
any recent authority directly in point concerning a solicitor's duty in
such circumstances?

   answer:
   time taken:

13. Farmer Giles has a livestock insurance policy on the life of his
farm animals, covering 'death through accident or disease'. One of
his cows broke a leg and Giles decided to slaughter it. He sold the
carcase to a butcher. He is now claiming under the policy. Advise the
insurers whether they are bound to pay up.

   answer:
   time taken:

14. Quadrat Printers printed and sold several thousand Christmas
cards last year. A lawyer who received one of these cards has written
to tell them that they are in danger of being prosecuted because they

did not print their name and address on the back of the card. Advise them if this is so.

answer:
time taken:

15. Sandy recently inherited a franchise to hold a market from his late uncle. The original grant of the franchise was made by royal patent in 1785. It has not been held for some years but when Sandy tried to revive it he was told by the local authority that he needed planning permission. Sandy claims that the Crown grant exempts him from the planning legislation. He has held the market on three occasions and has now received an enforcement notice from the local authority. He intends to disregard this. Is he able to?

answer:
time taken:

Chapter Nineteen

Suggested Solutions to Exercises

These solutions, up to date at the time of writing, may well be affected by later events. If your answer is more up to date, well done.

CHAPTER 1   EXERCISE A   SIMPLE FOCUSED PROBLEMS

All of the focused problems can be solved by judicious use of *Halsbury's Laws* index.

1.   *Halsbury's Laws* index: snipe, 2/327 (but actually 333 in the new volume): Wildlife and Countryside Act 1981, s. 2(4)(b): 1 February to 11 August.

2.   Yes: *Halsbury's Laws* index: 40/936: London Cab Order 1934 para. 35, amended by SI 1955/1853. *Halsbury's Statutory Instruments* 21/310.

3.   Never. *Halsbury's Laws* index: 9/1077 gives the old Coroners' Rules 1953/205, r. 15. *Supplement*: replaced by Coroners' Rules 1984/552, r. 18. (*Halsbury's Statutory Instruments* Vol. 5 gives these.) Rule 18: 'no inquest shall be held on a Sunday'.

4. Road Traffic Regulation Act 1984, s. 101 gives power of disposal. Details are in Removal and Disposal of Vehicles Regulations SI 1986 No. 183. Yes, once its licence has expired and they have tried and failed to find the owner. *Halsbury's Laws* index has it under Removal of Vehicles, giving Vol. 40, 328,331. Supplement has no changes relevant to powers of disposal.

5. Never (except for ice-cream chimes). Control of Pollution Act 1974, s. 62: not at all. Can be used outside the hours 9pm – 8am for some purposes but not for trade, advertising, etc. Supplement: no change.

6. Gas Quality Regulations 1972, reg. 7(1). Supp: replaced by SI 1983 No. 363, reg. 5: 'No person shall supply through pipes any gas that does not possess a distinctive smell'. *Halsbury's Laws* under 'smell'!

7. *Halsbury's Laws* Vol. 48 gives Registered Designs Act 1949, s. 8(1) = five years, plus two further five-year periods if applied for. But *Supplement* gives Copyright Designs and Patents Act 1988, s. 269 which inserts new s. 8 – 8B: = up to four more five-year periods. *Halsbury's Statutes* Vol. 33 gives only the old Act. *Supplement* gives existence of the new section. Text in *Current Service* vol. D: operative application (not grant) date: 1 August 1989.

8. *Halsbury's Laws* Vol. 48 (1984) gives Hallmarking Act 1973, s. 4 but nothing about this point. *Supplement* gives Hallmarking (Approved Hallmarks) Regulations 1986 SI 1986 No. 1757, reg. 2, which added s. 4(1A) = if weight of article less than four grams. In *Halsbury's Statutes* the 1973 Act is printed with amendments inserted.

9. Because Railway Clauses Consolidation Act 1845, s. 94 requires it. *Halsbury's Laws* index under 'milestone' – Vol. 38/890 (actually 889).

10. *Halsbury's Laws* index gives Driving Licence – refusal of – appeal against: 40/192 = may appeal to Magistrates' Court under Road Traffic Act 1972, s. 90(1), but this is out of date. The 1972 Act has been replaced by several Acts in 1988. *Supplement* does not have

an annotation to 192 but a quick scan gives other references to Road Traffic Act 1988. For example, para. 202 refers to para. 993D giving corresponding sections. This gives for 1972/90(1), RTA 1988, s. 100(1), (2). Service volume adds nothing.

CHAPTER 1   EXERCISE B   SIMPLE UNFOCUSED PROBLEMS

1. Sex discrimination is the underlying keyword. If we did not know the legislation, the Consolidated Index to *Halsbury's Laws* refers us to Vol. 16 (Employment, surprisingly) which at para. 771:2 summarises the Sex Discrimination Act 1975. After reading the general principles and the footnotes we might still be uncertain how these would apply to this case. But if we remembered to check the *Cumulative Supplement* we would find *James* v *Eastleigh Borough Council* [1990] 2 All ER 607; 3 WLR 55 (now 2 AC 751), in which the House of Lords held on facts similar to these that the local authority were discriminating against the man by conforming to the (admittedly sex-discriminatory) state pensionable ages.

2. *Halsbury's Laws* index under Competition – prize: see prize competition = Vol. 4 para. 151 = the old Act (1963). *Supplement* gives Lotteries and Amusements Act 1976. Section 14 says illegal and s. 23 definition includes the magazine. The new Vol. 4(1), published since the index, gives the 1976 Act and case law.

3. Town and Country Planning Act 1971, s. 55(6) gave defence for unauthorised works to a listed building where urgently needed in the interests of safety; with notice in writing to the authority as soon as reasonably practicable. Housing Act 1986, s. 40 by Sch. 9 para. 2 amended s. 55 by substituting a new subsection (6): requiring in addition to the s. 55 requirements, that it was not practicable to make temporary repairs, and that the works were the minimum necessary. The present Act, consolidating these, is the Planning (Listed Buildings and Conservation Areas) Act 1990, s. 9(3): see table of destinations. Is the 1990 Act in force? Section 94 says three months from date of passing (24 May 1990), so August 1990 commencement.

4. Wills Act 1837, s. 18: says a will is revoked by marriage. Law of Property Act 1925, s. 177 made an exception where a will was

expressed to be in contemplation of marriage. But *Re Coleman* [1976] Ch 1 gave s. 177 very restricted operation. So Administration of Justice Act 1982, (AJA) s. 18 repealed s. 177, giving freer interpretation possibilities. But AJA and repeal do not affect a will made before the commencement of AJA. AJA got Royal Assent October 1982 but commencement section s. 72(1) does not list s. 18, therefore it commences by s. 76(11): 1 January 1983. Peter's will was made November 1982 so is not saved. There is only the ineffective s. 177 to prevent automatic revocation, so Jane's claim is likely to fail.

5. *Halsbury's Laws* index gives 'flowerpot' in Vol. 40. That gives the Town Police Clauses Act 1847, s. 28: it is an offence, to the danger of residents or passengers in the street, to place any flower pot or box in an upper window without sufficiently guarding it against being blown down. Fine on level three. The Act by s. 28 gave power of arrest without warrant, but this was repealed by the Police and Criminal Evidence Act 1984, Sch. 7, leaving it within the general provisions of s. 25 where general arrest conditions apply. Probably none are applicable here, so the arrest itself may be unlawful.

CHAPTER 3   EXERCISE C   STATUTES

1. (a)   Sunday Observance Act 1780.
   (b)   Unsolicited Goods and Services Act 1971.
   (c)   Short Titles Act 1896.

2. (a)   Yes: in force on 31 July 1989.
   (b)   No: repealed by Statute Law Repeals Act 1989.
   (c)   Yes: 31 July 1990.
   (d)   1 January 1993 is commencement date.

3. Death.

4. Using their name, uniform, badge, except when play acting.

5. Any marriage by descendants of George II unless with the Sovereign's consent.

6. 'Married Women and Lunatics'.

CHAPTER 4   EXERCISE D   LAW REPORTS

1. *Butterworths' Company Law Cases, British Company Law Cases, Butterworths' Workmen's Compensation Cases, Western Weekly Reporter, Coke's Reports, Weekly Notes, Northern Ireland Law Reports, Commercial Cases, Estates Gazette, Simon's Tax Cases.*

2. Nine are listed in the *Citator* volume.

3. (a) *Lang* v *Jones and Skinner* [1992] 2 Current Law 414 (February); (1991) 10 Tr. LR 113.
    (b) *Sen* v *Headley* [1990] 2 WLR 620.
    (c) *Bristol Airport* v *Powdrill* [1990] Ch 744.
    (d) *R* v *Preston, The Times,* 13 May 1992.

4. Oil.

5. 1989 *CLYB* under Ecclesiastical law 1301 gives *Re Church Norton Churchyard* [1989] 3 WLR 272.

CHAPTER 5   EXERCISE E   STATUTORY INSTRUMENTS FAMILIARITY

1. Blue-eared pig disease, restrictions on movement, etc. The SI was amended by 1991/1992.

2. Three: SI 1989 No. 206 Access to Personal Files (Social Services) Regulations 1989, text in *Halsbury's Statutory Instruments* additional texts; SI 1989 No. 503 Access to Personal Files (Housing) Regulations 1989, summary only, in *Monthly Survey*; SI 1991 No. 1587 regulations amending SI 1989 No. 206, summarised in *Monthly Survey.*

3. The Land Registration Rules 1925, in *Halsbury's Statutory Instruments* under 'Real Property'. Various cases in recent years. Most recent *Belcourt* v *Belcourt* [1989] 2 All ER 34, on rule 301. Found by scanning the rules in *Halsbury's Statutory Instruments* and *Service,* or via the red and pink indexes.

4. Order in Council of 19 May 1671, which regulates appeals to the Privy Council from Jersey: the first SI in the chronological list in Vol. 1 of *Halsbury's Statutory Instruments* loose-leaf Service.

CHAPTER 6 EXERCISE F WORDS AND PHRASES

1. (a) *Dyer* v *Dorset County Council* [1988] 3 WLR 213.
   (b) *Dean* v *Upton, The Times* 10 May 1990 (CA).
   (c) *A-G* v *Brotherton* [1989] 2 All ER 423.
   (d) *Paul* v *DPP* (1990) 90 Cr App R 173 (DC).

2. Yes: *Peard* v *Johnes* Cro. Car. 382 (law dictionaries).

3. Yes: *R* v *Newcastle Licensing Committee* [1977] 1 WLR 1135 (CA) (law dictionaries).

4. Cp. *Re Arbib and Class's Contract* [1891] 1 Ch 601 at 613: probably not a sufficient 'return' but *obiter* because a stay of six months was held sufficient and it was not a will case (law dictionaries).

5. *De Souza* v *Home and Overseas Insurance, The Times* 19 September 1990 (CA): claim on these facts failed. (*CLYB* and *DLRI* give it under insurance, etc. It is not easily found as words and phrases, since it is not reported. (LEXIS has transcripts of CA cases.)

CHAPTER 8 EXERCISE G KEY WORDS

1. The essential aspect with which the law is concerned is conduct in the street: Street Collections (Metropolitan Police District) Regulations 1979/1230 (*Halsbury's Statutory Instruments* under 'Police'):

reg. 4. No collection without permit from the Commissioner of Police;

reg. 8. Each person must be in possession of written authority of promoter;

regs 10, 11. Must not importune, annoy, passersby;

reg. 12. Must remain stationary; no two collectors closer than 25 metres;
reg. 13. No one under 16 to collect;
reg. 14. No animals;
reg. 15. Collecting boxes to be numbered.

Many of these conditions can be waived by certificate from the Chief Superintendent where the collectors are carol singers but such waiver covers only 1–24 December. *Supplement*: no change.

2. Classify: conduct of meetings – local government. *Halsbury's Laws* index gives meetings – local authority, see Local Authority. That gives meetings – voting at – Vol. 28. That gives Local Government Act 1972, sch. 12. Para. 39 says chairman has a casting vote in addition to own vote. Supplement to para. 1122 gives *R v Bradford City Council ex p. Corris* [1989] 3 All ER 156. CA: the person presiding can use a casting vote as he sees fit in the best interests of those affected by it.

3. *Halsbury's Laws* index gives pilotage – compulsory: vol. 43, para. 868 which says the owner or master remains liable to anyone harmed by negligent navigation of a ship under pilotage, since the Pilotage Act 1913, s. 15 (repealed and re-enacted by Pilotage Act 1983, s. 35, which in turn was repealed and re-enacted by Pilotage Act 1987, s. 16.)

The paragraph does not deal with the liability of the pilot or his employers to the shipowner. The *Cumulative Supplement* gives *Esso v Hall Russell* [1989] AC 643, holding that the authority employing the pilot is not vicariously liable for him because he is an independent professional acting as a principal, not as a servant. (The hospital cases were distinguished.) Presumably the pilot can be personally liable so perhaps only insured pilots are now taken on board?

CHAPTER 8   EXERCISE H   CONCEALED KEYWORDS

1. The operative word is 'board'. See Rent Act 1977, s. 7(1) as interpreted in *Otter* v *Norman* [1989] AC 129; [1988] 3 WLR 321; 2 All ER 897 where the House of Lords agreed that providing just

continental breakfast was 'board' and this took the letting outside all the statutory provisions. However, a mere early morning cup of tea would not be sufficient, apparently; so probably free drinks from a machine would not suffice either, especially as there is no personal serving or housekeeping chore provided by the landlord, and the cost does not form a substantial proportion of the rent paid as indicated by s. 19.

2. If 'chiropractor' was a term unknown to you, a dictionary would be your first reference book. Then classify: VAT for medical services. (In a general work, is that VAT law or European law? Surprisingly the latter, because of VAT's origins.)

The vital term of art for VAT is 'supply': *Halsbury's Laws* Euro volume, Vol. 52 gives the Directive: 77/388/EEC, art. 13(A)(1)(C): medical care by medical and paramedical professions is an exempt supply, so Oscar should not have to charge. But check the *Supplement* to find a case on an osteopath: *Barkworth* v *Customs and Excise* [1988] STC 771: QBD upheld VAT Tribunal that the Directive leaves it to member states' definition of who is a paramedic. The UK criterion is statutory registration, and this does not apply to osteopaths, so the same would apply for chiropractors. An alternative route is to check *Current Law* and recent CLYBs. 1988 CLYB under VAT – exempt supply, gives six cases. This is 3617.

CHAPTER 9   EXERCISE I   UK JOURNALS

1. 'Education or Unpaid Labour?' by S. Dyer 138 *New Law Journal* 269.

2. (a)   *Insolvency Intelligence* 1992, part 5(2) has article by Higham about the unreported case of *Compaq Computer* v *Abercorn Ltd.*

   (b)   'Dangerous Dogs: a Problem Solved?' by Jeffreys (1990) 154 *Justice of the Peace* 225.

   (c)   For fetus, LJI prefers 'foetus' and then cross-refers to embryology. Looking back through this and last year's turns up Wells' article in 141 NLJ 1046.

3.   To the end of April 1992, 28 articles.

4.   Case note in 14 EIPR 24 by Glick and Page.

5.   Bill Thomas in [1991] *Legal Executive* 20.

CHAPTER 10   EXERCISE J   STATUTORY INSTRUMENTS

1.   Quite apart from any private law remedy Clarissa might have,
she can now invoke legislation which aims to deal with misleading
advertisements. If we did not know this, *Halsbury's Laws* index
under 'advertisement – misleading' directs us to Vol. 51 (a surprise:
the European Communities volume) at para. 8,92. That tells us there
was Council Directive 84/450 (for what this means see 14.1.10 below)
about misleading advertisements. Again, we need to check the
Supplement at that volume and paragraph number to find its
implementation: Control of Misleading Advertisements Regulations
1988, No. 915. The actual text can be found in *Halsbury's Statutory
Instruments*. Neither there nor in its annual supplement, however,
does it tell us whether these regulations have come before the courts
for interpretation; but we know how to find that out by other means:
the *Law Reports* index (the present year's and the ten-year volume,
though we only need the years since 1988) is the first place to check.
The alphabetical index of 'Statutory Instruments considered' gives
this SI as involved in *Director General of Fair Trading* v *Tobyward*
[1989] 1 WLR 517. If you found this you will know how relevant it is.

2.   *Consolidated Index* to *Halsbury's Statutory Instruments* gives it
under 'tomato ketchup'. Food Standards (Tomato Ketchup) Order
1949 (SI 1949 No. 1817) not less than six per cent tomato solids or
puree. May also have for flavouring: onion, garlic, spices. However,
at the time of writing the 1991 *Monthly Survey* (if not the annual
Supplement) shows that SI 1949 No. 817 is revoked by SI 1991 No.
1231. This is summarised in the *Monthly Survey* but it does not say
exactly what has been changed. In fact the old Order has gone
completely. Presumably new regulations under the Food Safety Act
1990 will follow.

3. *Consolidated Index* gives 'Hovercraft – liability – carriage of passengers and luggage' = Vol. 17 p. 310 = SI 1986 No. 1305, made under Hovercraft Act 1968 (former SI 1979 No. 305 revoked). Articles 3, 4 and 5 apply the Carriage by Air Act 1961 to passengers and their baggage (but not to their goods and vehicles, to which Carriage of Goods by Sea Act 1971 applies). Article 10 'for convenience' sets out the Acts with necessary modifications. 1961 Act, Sched. 1, art. 22 (as amended by SI 1987 No. 1835) makes it £80,009 for passenger injuries; and £246 for luggage in passenger's charge. Update: various new hovercraft SIs but only about pollution, equipment, etc.

4. *Consolidated Index* gives contact lenses – registered opticians – rules: 12,252 = General Optical Council (Contact Lens (Qualifications etc.) Rules Order of Council 1988, (r. 15) fitting must be accompanied by necessary instruction and information as to care, wear, treatment, cleaning and maintenance . . . and the person fitting such lenses shall be obliged to provide for clinical management and adjustment of the fitting for six months from the date of the first fitting. (Summary only in *Halsbury's Statutory Instruments* = 'six months of patient after care'.) SI 1989 No. 791 adds requirement that the optician must also give particulars necessary to enable the lenses to be replicated.

As for redress, Mary may complain to the Disciplinary Committee of the General Optical Council under the Opticians Act 1989. You could find this in *Halsbury's Laws* index; or get a strong hint from the SIs next to the Contact Lens Rules, which lay down the disciplinary procedure and refer to the 1989 Act.

5. This is a veritable treasure hunt. The Act says 'liable to a daily default fine' but does not say what it is. If the Queen's Printer's copy of the Act is being used, you must make intelligent use of its table of contents. Annotated statute directs to s. 430. That refers to Sch. 10 which says the fine is 'one-fiftieth of the statutory maximum'. The beginning of the schedule refers for the maximum to Magistrates Courts Act 1980, s. 32. Section 32 says the prescribed sum is £1000 unless increased by s. 143(1). Section 143(1) allows the Secretary of

State to increase fines to take account of the value of money. Criminal Penalties (Increase) Order 1984 (SI 1984 No. 447) doubled it to £2000. So one-fiftieth = £40 a day. But the Criminal Justice Act 1991, s. 17 increases the fine to £5000. Is it yet in force? See the Commencement Order 1992/333. Of course a fully up to date annotated statute or textbook will give just the current figure, thank goodness.

6.   Road Vehicles (Construction and Use) Regulations 1986 (SI 1986 No. 1078. Regulations 105 and 98 apply respectively. Both types of conduct are criminal. Since this is obviously magisterial law, the appropriate source is *Stone's Justices' Manual* under motor vehicle. *Halsbury's Statutory Instruments* set them out under Transport. *Halsbury's Laws* index indicates Vol. 40 as the appropriate volume for all traffic offences and the references can be found there.

7.   Outer Space Act 1986, s. 4(3)(d) and s. 11: apply to Secretary of State. Regulations: The Outer Space Act 1986 (Fees) Regulations 1989/1306: £1000. *Halsbury's Laws* index gives Vol. 18 (1977) = treaties only. *Supplement* gives the Act. The Act gives power to make regulations. *Halsbury's Statutory Instruments* index says 3,91. This gives a summary of the regulations. Various recent SIs under the Act extend it to e.g., Channel Islands and give exemptions for schools, etc.

8.   *Halsbury's Statutes* index 'Business Expansion' – eligible shares 44,349 = s. 290 (only about relief from tax). *Supplement* gives s. 290A in Vol. 43. The section inserted into the Income and Corporation Taxes Act 1988 by the Finance Act 1988, s. 51(1)(b) = £500,000. But see now the Business Expansion Scheme (Substitution of Permitted Maximum Amount) Order (SI 1990 No. 862) raising it to £750,000. (The scheme may end soon.)

9.   Courts and Legal Services Act 1990, s. 21 creates this Ombudsman. Section 22: powers to investigate 'professional body'; s. 22(11) says this is to be specified by the Lord Chancellor. Legal Services Ombudsman (Jurisdiction) Order (SI 1990 No. 2485) = General Council of the Bar, Law Society, Council for Licensed Conveyancers (as to the manner in which they have dealt with complaints).

10. *Halsbury's Statutory Instruments* gives Zebra crossings – see Pedestrian crossings, which refers to SI 1971 No. 1524, reg. 8. The notes give *M'Kerrell* v *Robertson* [1956] SC(J) 50 as authority that she is on the crossing for the purposes of precedence.

CHAPTER 11   EXERCISE K   *THE DIGEST*

1.   *Gill* v *El Vino* [1983] 1 QB 425 (CA).

The difficulty in finding this case is that the index does not give 'wine bar' or 'public house'. It has 'licensed premises' but this does not lead anywhere useful. You just have to keep thinking of synonyms which the law recognises. You should eventually hit on 'inns and inn-keepers', which is in Vol. 29. Page 9 gives obligations to supply needs and remedies for refusal, but nothing about this case. But Vol. 29 is dated 1982 so you need to check the *Supplement*, which gives footnote 109a; the case in *Continuation* Vol. F.

2.   *Davis* v *Colchester City Hospital* [1933] 4 DLR 68.

This is fairly quick to find once you give up trying under 'Negligence' and resort to 'Medicine'.

3.   This does come under negligence, but the Negligence volume, Vol. 36(1), has no case more recent than the 1970s. The 1991 *Supplement* has *White* v *St Albans* as it appeared in *The Times* in 1990.

4.   *Haddon* v *Lynch* [1911] VLR 230, found under 'Nuisance'.

5.   *Company X* v *Switzerland* 16 ECHR Decisions 85. Within the scope of *The Digest* you should have realised this must come under European Law or Human Rights. As Switzerland is not in the EEC, it would have to be Human Rights, and there is only one volume for these, *Continuation* Vol. G. Browsing a few pages gives it as case 1101.

6.   The cases index volume gives *Street* v *Mountford* in *Continuation* Vol. G, 1703a of Vol. 31 (1). The *Cumulative Supplement* for 1991

gives many annotations. The latest are *Family Housing Association* v *Jones* and *McCarthy* v *Bence*, both 1990.

CHAPTER 12   EXERCISE L   FORMS AND PRECEDENTS

1.   *Encyclopaedia of Forms and Precedents* General index: film production, actor, engagement of, nudity 15,504. Vol. 15, para. 504 gives Equity agreement which requires the actors to have the script beforehand. The Equity agreement also controls access to the set, nudity at auditions, etc., and provides for destruction of all unused material. Among clauses in the contract is cl. 19 of form 36: compulsory destruction of unused parts, but stills can be used by the company, subject to the artists' consent; and they can only reject a limited amount (e.g., 50 per cent) of material.

2.   General index under 'disinterment' gives 6/522: application to the Home Office E4 Division for licence. Fee £10. *Supplement*: nothing relevant.

3.   *Encyclopaedia* index: highway – stopping-up, refers to Vol. 18, Form 143: request under Highways Act 1980, s. 117 as amended, to highway authority for them in turn to request the magistrates under s. 116 to make an order. Request should have a plan attached and outline details of the proposed manner of stopping it up.

CHAPTER 14   EXERCISE M   EUROPEAN COMMUNITY LAW

1.   Regulations 1686/75 maintains 1295/75. That is a regulation controlling the importation into Germany and Benelux of Korean synthetic socks. Both regulations are spent.

Regulation 87/153 is a guideline for additives in animal foods. It is still in force.

Regulation 3104/87 amends reg. 1569/77. That is about the procedure for taking over cereals by intervention agencies. *Current*

Status Supplement says 3104 is ssd (superseded) by Regulation 1022/90. Regulation 1022/90 is still in force.

2. Regulation 3626/82 is the regulation for the implementation of the Convention on International Trade in endangered species. The case of *Commission* v *France* C 182/89 (1990) Transcript 29, not yet reported, is an interpretation of the regulation.

3. *Commission* v *Luxembourg and Belgium* [1962] ECR 425; [1963] CMLR 199.

4. The Act itself gives it: 85/374/EEC. With the year known it can be found in the *Methodological Table* for 1985: Vol. 28 L206-218. Signed by J. Poos.

5. Yes: 91/157. This is given in the index to *Current Status*. Vol. 2 gives the Directive: OJ L78, p. 38. (Appears in *Current Law* for 1991 under Consumer Protection.) To be complied with by 18 September 1992, but there has been no UK implementation yet?

6. *Consorzio d'Abruzzo* v *European Commission* [1988] CMLR 841. If you know the approximate year, the simplest way is to scan CLYB for a couple of years, under European Communities – decisions – withdrawals. The Advocate-General was J. Mischo.

7. Directive 89/629 of 4 December 1989 provides for the reduction of noise from subsonic civil aircraft, by the legal requirement of a noise certificate to show the plane's conformity with International Convention, with various exemptions. Member states must comply by 30 September 1990. Found in subject index to *Current Status*, or in *Directory of Community Legislation in Force* analytical register (Vol. I) under Transport policy and also under Environment. *Implementator* does not list it, surprisingly. CLYB 1990 under Aviation gives Air Navigation (Noise Certification) Order 1990/1514. *Halsbury's Statutory Instruments* only has a summary but *Halsbury's Laws* sets it out without however mentioning the Directive. (Hence the failure of the *Implementator* to mention it). It is clear that part of the Order is implementing the Directive. A UK operator

would probably be aware of the Order without knowing or needing to know of the Directive.

CHAPTER 15   EXERCISE N   FOREIGN AND INTERNATIONAL LAW

1.   *Bowman and Harris* Supplement shows that the 1980 Agreement has expired. It is replaced by the 1986 Agreement. The UK is a party to it. It contains certain provisions for price stabilisation and adjustment.

2.   Index to *Bowman and Harris* gives it under 'Olympic' = Treaty 808 = Nairobi Treaty of 1981. This prevents the registration of the olympic symbol as a trade mark or sign for commercial purposes. The UK appears not to be a party. Presumably our trade mark etc. law is thought a sufficient safeguard?

3.   None. The presence or absence of a seal has no effect on legality. See *Martindale-Hubbell*.

4.   It is a criminal offence to send dangerous goods in a vessel under a false description: Merchant Shipping Act, s. 446(1). Section 448 says the Master is entitled to throw them overboard, and is not liable for doing so. See also Carriage of Goods by Sea Act 1971, s. 1(2) and *Hague-Visby* Rules, art. IV(6).

Halsbury's Laws 43 para. 788, n. 4 suggests that since under *Hague-Visby* Rules, art. III(2) there is an obligation to properly and carefully keep and discharge goods carried, this requires the Master to act reasonably, if there is no immediate danger. But art. III(2) is expressly stated to be 'subject to art. IV'. Update: nothing relevant in *Supplement*.

5.   The Brussels Convention governs the jurisdiction of the courts of the Community to hear international disputes. It is incorporated into UK law by the Civil Jurisdiction and Judgments Act 1982. The Convention is scheduled to the Act.

The basic principle (art. 2), is that a party domiciled in a Community country should only be sued before the courts of that country. Under art. 53 a corporation or association is domiciled where its 'seat' is, according to the rules of private international law of that country. According to s. 42, a company is domiciled in UK if either it is incorporated here and has its registered office here, or has its central management or control here. We can assume that Bell & Lever are based in UK and that Klang is incorporated in Germany and so domiciled there. (It is possible that German conflicts rules would say that Klang is domiciled in London since it has an office there, but this seems doubtful. Remember the presumption that in the absence of evidence, the foreign law is the same as English law!)

It follows that on the face of it Klang are correct. This is further borne out by art. 5 which says that the courts of the place of performance have jurisdiction. However, there could be argument here that the place of performance is England, allowing for proceedings here. (There are various cases on the application of this article.) The counterclaim point is fallacious. Art. 6 allows a counterclaim in proceedings irrespective of whether the same matter could have been initiated in that country, not being the counterclaimed party's domicile.

6. (a) The Brussels Convention (see previous answer): since the party to be sued here is not domiciled in any contracting state, art. 4 says that the rules of jurisdiction in force in the contracting state involved (i.e., France) apply. That includes the 'exorbitant' rules which are precluded as between contracting states by art. 3, e.g., in France, arts 14 and 15 of their Civil Code (which say what?) and in England such rules as e.g., our taking jurisdiction if the defendant has property here.

Assuming France's rules accept England as an appropriate forum in these circumstances, the action can be brought here. As it falls outside the Convention, England would accept jurisdiction in accordance with ordinary conflict of laws principles, e.g., proper law of the contract, place of performance, if defendants have property here, etc.

(b) The Rome Convention: this is the EEC Convention on the Law Applicable to Contractual Obligations. It is designed to harmonise the rules of conflicts of laws in contracts among the EC countries, to prevent forum shopping and increase legal certainty. It is incorporated into UK law by the Contracts (Applicable Law) Act 1990 and scheduled thereto.

Article 3 says that a contract shall be governed by the law chosen by the parties. They are free to choose. If therefore the matter is litigated in an English court bound by the new Act (is it in force?), the Convention would accept the parties' choice of law.

7.   As Poland is not in the EEC and this sounds very recent, the best place to check is *European Current Law*. This gives the answer in the January part: 40m zlotys.

CHAPTER 16   EXERCISE O   LEXIS

1.   The hard-copy approach would be to classify this under planning control, and specifically advertising. (It could also be aviation: the Air Navigation Order 1972 (SI 1972 No. 66) forbids any such advertisement above 60 metres high.) There are various planning regulations. One of these, SI 1984 No. 421 (now revoked) regulates balloon advertisements. One of its preconditions, that the balloon be attached to the site, was interpreted in the case of *Wadham Stringer* v *Fareham BC* (1986) 53 P & CR 336; 85 LGR 776 (DC) to include where it is attached to a vehicle on the site.

The LEXIS approach, after some preliminary analysis, would be a search of the STATIS file for any Acts or SIs: control! w/15 advertisement! or some such strategy would find the regulations. But because balloon is an unusual word in the law, it would be worth adding this either by modifying or with the 'focus' command. It would then be useful to check the CASES file to see if the regulation had been before the courts. This could be discovered simply by putting in its name, or number, plus the date. Even more directly, however, balloon w/50 advertisement! should do it.

2.   The hard-copy approach: books on Landlord & Tenant can be searched under Covenant. A little patient scanning of *Hill and Redman*, for example, will produce at 1-2591 the case of *Field* v *Barkworth* [1986] 1 All ER 362. This holds that a ban on subletting

etc., 'part' must imply a ban on the whole. It is also in *Halsbury's Laws* under Landlord and Tenant.

By LEXIS, whatever search strategy one adopts (e.g., covenant! AND sublet! w/20 part) produces very many cases and it is hard to refine the search effectively. Scrolling through the lot will eventually produce the case but traditional searching is much quicker.

The moral: LEXIS is usually much quicker, at least when you have first done your ground clearing and devised a sensible strategy before starting, but it is not so good where all the keywords are commonplace legal terms occurring in countless cases; Whereas the practised human eye can scan columns of relevant text and footnotes accurately and rapidly.

CHAPTER 18   EXERCISE P   FINAL SELF-ASSESSMENT TEST

1. See the commencement section at end of Act: two months from the date of passing = 1 November 1990 plus two months = 1 January 1991.

Time: 2 minutes.

2. Act of that name found in indexes of *Stone's Justices Manual, Halsbury's Laws*, etc. As amended, = level three on standard scale. This refers to the Criminal Justice Act 1982, s. 38 which, as amended by the Criminal Penalties (Increase) Order 1984, is £400. But *Halsbury's Statutes* noter-up to the 1982 Act warns you that this will be increased to £1000 when the Criminal Justice Act 1991, s. 17 is brought into effect. So this must be checked.

Time: $4\frac{1}{2}$ minutes.

3. You were told '1990' so provided you recognise the area as one of trade description, *Current Law Year Book, Halsbury's Annual Abridgment, Daily Law Reports Index* for that year all give *Hurley v Martinez and Co.* (DC)

Time: $2\frac{1}{4}$ minutes.

4. Find in the numerical list in *Halsbury's Statutory Instruments* service volume. If it is not yet in the full list at the beginning, check the monthly survey to get the subject heading and look at the numerical list there: dogs' droppings in public places were brought under the Environmental Protection Act.

Time: 2 minutes.

5. *White Book*: There is no Order 84.

Time: 40 seconds.

6. 'Pannage' is obviously a legal term of art which needs looking up. *Halsbury's Laws* gives it but is uninformative. Check in either *Words and Phrases* or *Stroud's*. Both give it as a right to have one's pigs go into the woods of another and eat acorns and beech mast but only *fallen* from the trees and lying on the ground – and no shaking the trees! *Chilton* v *London Corporation* (1878) 7 Ch D at 565.

Time: 2¼ minutes.

7. Says 'form' so *Encyclopaedia of Forms and Precedents* general index: 'zoo' gives 2, 906 and 907 = application to local authority. Licence lasts for four years initially.

Time: 1¼ minutes.

8. Case name but no reference so you can can check in *Current Law Case Citator* (because though this is an old case it remains important and must have been cited in the last half century); or case index to *Halsbury's Laws*, or *Digest*. These give the report's references. The solicitors appear at the end: Bower and Cotton, and Pritchard Englefield and Co.

Time: 2 minutes.

9. Latest case in DLRI is *Chase Manhattan Equities Ltd* v *Goodman, The Times*, 23 May 1991.

Time: 3½ minutes.

10. 'Aumbry' was an unknown term to you, presumably? It is not in the law dictionaries either. General index to *Halsbury's Laws* gives it, and 'legality' 14,965. = yes: if the sacrament is reserved with the bishop's approval because an aumbry is not regarded as an ornament (which therefore might be questionable) but simply as a cupboard.

Time: 1½ minutes.

11. *Law Commission* No. 191, published in 1990: 'Risk of Damage after Contract for Sale'. If your library has all the Commission's reports filed together, a look through should find it assuming your holding is complete. The Commission also publishes lists of reports. However a more certain way is to check *Current Law* and recent CLYBs under 'Law Reform'. 1990 CLYB gives it at paragraph 2878.

Time: 1¾ minutes.

12. *Edwards* v *Lee*, 30 October 1991; 141 *NLJ* 1517, Brooke J held that a solicitor has a duty of care under the *Hedley Byrne* 'special relationship' and the third party is entitled to rely on the reference. *Current Law* 1991 index under Solicitor – misleading statements – character reference.

Time: 2½ minutes.

13. *Halsbury's Laws* Vol. 25, Insurance: para. 683: if an animal is slaughtered through motives of humanity following an accident, that is regarded as fatal injury caused by the accident, but it must be reasonable to slaughter, for purposes of avoiding unnecessary suffering. *Obiter* in *Shiells* v *Scottish Assurance* (1889) 16 R (Ct of Sess.) 1014 at 1019. *Supplement* and *Noter-up*: nothing further. Presumably the insured will have to bring into account any amount he received for the carcase.

Time: 3 minutes.

14. *Halsbury's Laws* index: Printer, name and address, printing of: 37,1012. This gives the Newspapers, Printers and Reading Rooms Repeal Act 1869, s. 1: if the matter printed is meant to be published and dispersed, it must have the name and address of the printer. . . .

Otherwise a fine of £25 – for each copy printed! But the Printers Imprint Act 1961, s.1(1)(a) says that these provisions do not apply unless the matter printed is words grouped together to convey a message other than words calculated to convey only a greeting, invitation or other message in a conventional form, so greetings cards appear to be exempt. The offence is only prosecutable by a Law Officer.

Time: 4 minutes.

15.   The case on these facts is *Spook Erection Ltd* v *Secretary of State* [1989] QB 300 (CA). It can be found by trying the various keywords in *Halsbury's Laws* index. Market – Crown, grant by, gives Vol. 29,604. Vol. 29 is dated 1979, so a check of the supplement under that paragraph gives the case. Or it can be found in the index under Planning permission – Crown land which gives Vol. 46,94. Vol. 46 (about to be reissued) is dated 1984. Para. 94, note 20, on the old Act, is picked up by the *Supplement* which gives the *Spook* case. This says that the owner of a franchise from the Crown is not acting on behalf of the Crown so as to be exempt from the requirement of planning consent.

Time: 3¼ minutes

If you took much longer than these timings, or failed to get some of the answers, you need not feel downcast. Your skill must already have greatly improved. It will continue to do so if you keep it exercised. It is worth trying to research frequently – for other people if necessary – if only to maintain your familiarity with the sources and tools. Your skill in choosing an appropriate line of inquiry, and in pursuing it methodically, will come with practice, and you will anyway with specialisation come to move easily in your chosen area of law and its own special sources.

Select Bibliography

GENERAL WORKS

Most of the guides to legal research on offer in this country are aimed at student beginners in law and do not extend beyond the sort of academic materials that they need to handle. The few more advanced or more comprehensive books include:

Dane and Thomas: *How to Use a Law Library* (Sweet & Maxwell). For many of the sources I have described this gives a much fuller account, with well illustrated detail. At the time of writing, however, the current edition (1987) is rather dated.

Holborn: *Butterworths' Guide to Legal Research* (forthcoming 1992).

Jeffries and Miskin: *Legal Research in England and Wales* (1991) comes from the publishers of DLRI and LJI, Legal Information Resources Ltd, Blackshawhead, W. Yorks, and is a very useful survey of the main sources. Librarians speak highly of it. Lawyers seem hardly to know it.

Jeffries: *Legal Research and the Law of the European Communities* (1990) is from the same publisher with a similar approach to the sources but a much more critical attitude, reflecting the frustrations which even the most experienced and informed researchers encounter when trying to penetrate the EC's labyrinth.

Logan: *Information Sources in Law* (Butterworths, 1986) is in many academic libraries. It is not as useful for present purposes as its title promises, consisting of bibliographic essays by specialist contributors each introducing the literature of a general subject area.

Other common law countries have produced introductions to legal research. There are some excellent American works, but the nature and organisation of US law makes these of comparatively little relevance to us. Australia and Canada have produced books which, while concentrating on their own law, have some coverage of UK law; and also have given some attention to technique. The following can be found in academic libraries:

Campbell and others: *Legal Research Materials and Methods* (Law Book Co., Sydney, Australia, 1988).

Fong and Ellis: *Finding the Law* (Legal Information Press, Sydney, Australia, 1990).

MacEllven: *Legal Research Handbook* (Butterworths, Toronto, Canada, 1986).

SPECIFIC TOOLS

Among the most useful are:

Raistrick: *Index to Legal Citations and Abbreviations* (Professional Books, Abingdon, 1981).

Sweet and Maxwell's *Guide to Law Reports and Statutes* (4th ed. 1962).

Bieber's *Dictionary of Legal Abbreviations: reference guide for attorneys, legal secretaries, paralegals and law students* (Hein, Buffalo, N.Y., 1988). You will have guessed that this is mainly American. It does also contain some UK references.

William C. Burton's *Legal Thesaurus* (Macmillan, New York, 1980) is the most comprehensive English word list for lawyers, helping us to paraphrase and to find synonyms or associated words for use in researching.

The *Eurovoc Thesaurus*, companion volumes to the OJ, are arranged alphabetically and by subject and are multilingual, so a help in classifying and finding terms and concepts which EC law recognises.

Euroconfidential publish two very useful reference directories: *Directory of EC Information Sources* and *Directory of European Institutions*. These together give a mass of information on all the officialdom of the EC, its agencies, representatives, repositories.

Nichols: *Aslib Law Databases* (1991) is a very useful list of all known UK and international on-line services which have any legal content, with descriptions of coverage, cost, etc.